Essential Lutheranism

Theological Perspectives
on
Christian Faith and Doctrine

Carl E. Braaten

American Lutheran Publicity Bureau
Delhi, New York

Cover: Christian Beyer reading the German text of the *Augsburg Confession* before the Emperor Charles V and assembled dignitaries on June 25, 1530 at 3 PM in the chapter-room of the bishop's palace. Wood-cut by an unknown 16th century artist in Nürnberg.

The American Lutheran Publicity Bureau wishes to acknowledge with deep appreciation the work of Gregory Fryer, William Fensterer and Dorothy Zelenko in their proofreading of the text, Josh Messner for artwork and cover design, and Martin A. Christiansen for internal layout and design work.

Frederick J. Schumacher
Executive Director, ALPB

ISBN 1-892921-22-7

American Lutheran Publicity Bureau
PO Box 327
Delhi, NY 13753

Carl E. Braaten, *Essential Lutheranism: Theological Perspectives on Christian Faith and Doctrine* (Delhi, NY: ALPB Books, 2012), 206 pp.

To my friends and colleagues

in

The Society of the Holy Trinity

Contents

Preface

In this preface I will present a few reflections on the whence and whither of my thinking as a theologian standing within the Lutheran tradition of the Christian faith. It all began in my childhood years growing up in a missionary colony on the island of Madagascar. The Lutheran mission in Madagascar was first started by missionaries from Norway in the middle of the nineteenth century. That was followed by a strong contingency of Norwegian American missionaries in the 1880s. My parents were sent to Madagascar by the mission board of the Norwegian Lutheran Church in America. I experienced four different national influences — American, Norwegian, French, and Malagasy.

In 150 years the Lutheran Church that the Norwegian and American missionaries planted in Madagascar has grown to three and a half million members (3,500,000). It is among the ten largest Lutheran churches in the world, larger than the Lutheran Church–Missouri Synod. And like the Lutheran Churches in Ethiopia and Tanzania, it continues to grow at a steady rate. The Christian Church in Madagascar was born and baptized in the blood of the martyrs. Queen Ranavalona I condemned the spread of the gospel. Christians were persecuted and killed. Bibles were burned. Worship assemblies were outlawed. When the Queen died, she was replaced by a king friendly to the spread of Christianity. The birth of the church in Madagascar is a microcosm of the rise and expansion of Christianity in the early centuries, from being a persecuted church of the martyrs in the Roman Empire to becoming the established church of Christendom in the Holy Roman Empire.

The Norwegian immigrants came to America without a lot of baggage. In their wooden trunks they might have packed a copy of Johann Arndt's *True Christianity*, a book of devotions, Luther's *Small Catechism*, a Bible, and perhaps a hymn book. These would have to do the job of transmitting the Christian faith and the Lutheran tradition to the new country. The Norwegian Lutherans who settled predominantly in the midwest were a mixed bag. In 1900 there were fourteen different synods among Norwegian Lutherans. They disputed over polity, doctrine, and ritual. In 1917 a miracle of sorts happened. Three different types of Norwegian Lutherans merged to become the Norwegian Lutheran Church in America. One was a group of pietists who reflected the Haugean tradition. They started Augsburg College. A second was an orthodox group that belonged to the Norwegian Synod. They started Luther College. A third was a moderate group that worked for the union of Norwegian Lutherans. They started St. Olaf College. Three Lutheran Colleges within a hundred miles of each other represented three different streams of Lutheran piety, doctrine, worship, and lifestyle.

I met a lot of Lutheran Haugeaners in Minnesota and South Dakota. They had a well-deserved reputation of being legalists and pietists. The daughter of one of these pietists told me that she was not allowed to pick up a needle on Sunday. The Haugeaners were named after Hans Nielsen Hauge, a lay revivalist preacher in Norway in the early nineteenth century. He attacked the established State Church of Norway for its dead orthodoxy, formalistic liturgies, pompous vestments, and authoritarian governance. This kind of pietism was, of course, not invented in Norway. Hauge and his fellow pietists shared with all the Nordic countries a common genealogy that stemmed from Germany, including such notables as Johann Arndt, Philipp Jacob Spener, August Hermann Francke, and Count Ludwig von Zinzendorf. About the same time that Hans Nielsen Hauge was traveling around Norway preaching his evangelistic message, Carl Olaf Rosenius in Sweden, Erik Pontoppidan in Denmark, and Paavo Ruotsalainen in Finland were doing the same kind of itinerant revivalist preaching in their respective countries. Their message emphasized pretty much the same things: the centrality of the laity in the church, congregational freedom, pious living, and self-discipline.

In Norway the State Church was afraid of the populism of Hauge and his rhetorical power to stir the emotions of the common folks. So the State Church prohibited lay preaching and prayer meetings in private homes, and on several occasions the authorities threw Hauge into jail. Long after his death the spirit of Hans Nielsen Hauge lived on into the twentieth century in midwest Lutheranism. However, through the process of translation his message of revival all too often got boiled down to the big four "No's": no dancing, no drinking, no smoking, no cards.

The Lutheran missionaries I grew up with were all pietists, but their pietism was tempered by a great deal of pragmatism and common sense demanded by the tough conditions of living on the frontiers of pioneer evangelistic work. Haugean pietism was something else. Ole Hallesby was the most famous Norwegian theologian of the twentieth century in the line of Haugean pietism. In 1953 he delivered a speech over the radio. I was a student at Luther Seminary in St. Paul at the time, and I recall that it caused something of a buzz. He said on the air: "How can you who are unconverted lie down calmly to sleep at night, when you don't know if you will wake up in your bed or in hell? If you dropped dead in your sleep this moment, you would go straight to hell." The Bishop of Hamar, Kristian Schelderup, responded for the more liberal side, stating that the idea of damnation to hell is incompatible with a religion of love. The people were polled for their opinions. The majority said they believed there was a hell, but they did not like preaching that scared the hell out of people.

Norwegian Lutherans earned a reputation for their doctrinal disputes, often so bitterly fought that it split communities and families. The high church Lutherans of the old Norwegian Synod did not get along with the low church Lutherans of the Hauge Synod, and their heirs still don't much like each other. In 1948 the Norwegian Lutheran Church in America changed its name to the Evangelical Lutheran Church. The leaders engaged in a heated debate at Central Lutheran Church in Minneapolis. Some wanted to get rid of the "Norwegian" label, because such a specific ethnic identity would inhibit evangelism and church growth among people not of Norwegian descent. Others wanted to keep the name "Norwegian" because once the church goes down the slippery slope of accommodating American culture, who knows where it will end up.

The Norwegian color of the church in which I grew up has faded away. I do not lament that. The question is whether the Lutheran substance is being lost in the melting pot of post-denominational liberal Protestantism in America. This is a theological question that all Lutherans in America face, whether in the Evangelical Lutheran Church in America (ELCA) or in the Lutheran Church–Missouri Synod. The same question must be of equally grave concern *mutatis mutandis* of all other Lutheran church bodies, synods, or sects. When I decided to become a theologian, I never had any other intention but to become the best Lutheran theologian I could be. My education was Lutheran in spades. I was graduated from a Lutheran High School, Augustana Academy, in Canton, South Dakota. Then I was graduated with a philosophy major from St. Olaf College in Northfield, Minnesota. The name sounds Catholic, but it was 100% Lutheran. After three years at Luther Seminary in St. Paul, Minnesota, I moved way beyond the orbit of midwest Norwegian Lutheran pietism. I had a pretty definite feeling that is not where I could end up theologically with sustainable commitment and integrity.

This book is a product of the long journey that has taken me to a theological outlook that I — as well as others — call "evangelical catholic." I would like to believe that it is a growing movement within world Lutheranism, but I am not sure. In any case, my conviction is not dependent on any consideration of actual numbers or potential success. To use the current jargon, "It is what it is." The many years of study at the

10

Universities of Paris, Harvard, Heidelberg, and Oxford did not cause me to forget or forsake my roots in the Norwegian Lutheran mission in Madagascar. They nourished me spiritually and kept me focussed on the essentials of Christian faith and doctrine. Anyone who knows what they are will see their effects reflected in most everything I have written, especially the books on Lutheran identity, Christology, the gospel of salvation, justification by faith, the mission of world evangelization, and so forth. These enduring core beliefs and doctrines rooted in the missionary situation have made me averse to the trends that American religion accommodates, aka gnosticism, that spawns the various heresies and syncretisms that have captured the main institutions of Lutheranism today, its bureaucracies, educational institutions, and publishing houses.

I do not believe in raising the white flag of surrender. As Yogi Berra said, "It ain't over till it's over!" My wife, LaVonne, keeps reminding me of the pendulum theory. Church history is full of examples of dramatic reversals of the way things are that no one expected. The dawn brings forth glimmerings of light after the darkest of nights. Like the Dow Jones, it can plummet down one day and bounce back the next. We live by hope, not fatalistically riveted to the way things are. In any case, we have no choice. We cannot re-invent ourselves and look around for a different spiritual home and theological identity. Some seem to be able to do that. I cannot, having been so thoroughly marinated in the juices of the Lutheran traditions of Christianity. As Luther said, "I cannot do otherwise. So help me God!"

This book aims to present the essentials of confessional Lutheran theology in an ecumenical and pluralistic age. I do not believe that any old kind of Lutheranism will do. There are heretical and apostate forms of Lutheranism evident for all eyes to see. Many of the German Christians in Hitler's Nazi regime were Lutherans. Bearing the name "Lutheran" is no guarantee of being faithful to the gospel of Jesus Christ. I do not want to teach Lutheran theology at the cost of being biblically Christian, or at the cost of being evangelical, catholic, or orthodox. To be a confessional Lutheran today is to be evangelical, in radical distinction from being some kind of liberal or mainline Protestant, to be catholic in the sense of belonging to the body of Christ spread throughout the world on a mission to preach the gospel to the nations, without narrowing the meaning down to being "Roman," and to be orthodox with a strong sense of continuity with the great tradition of the church founded on the apostles, the church fathers, the ancient creeds, without any romantic infatuation with Eastern Orthodoxy, its rites and icons. I do not want to encourage any kind of sectarian Lutheranism in an ecumenical age. There are few signs in the official expressions of the Lutheran Churches in America, whether on the left or the right, that they are evangelical with a passion for global evangelization, or that they are catholic with an ecumenical vision of the whole church of Christ on earth, or that they are orthodox with a strong sense of continuity with church tradition antecedent to the Reformation.

Looking around we see roughly three alternative models of Lutheranism in America today. The first type aims to be gnesio-Lutheran, that is, to be authentically Lutheran by appealing to the *Book of Concord* and the period of seventeenth century scholastic orthodoxy. The end result of such an exclusive stress on the Lutheran confessional heritage is to narrow down the meaning of Lutheranism to what makes it utterly different from all other church traditions, especially the Reformed Protestant to the one side and the Roman Catholic to the other side. This approach tends to be anti-ecumenical; its clearest expression can be seen within the Lutheran Church–Missouri Synod and the Wisconsin Evangelical Lutheran Synod.

A second type of Lutheranism is motivated by various social agendas; it finds allies among the peace and justice advocates inspired mostly by liberal, left-wing, liberationist theologies. This approach is ecumenically yoked with all of the mainline liberal Protestant denominations. Its clearest expression is the Evangelical Lutheran Church in America. Twenty-five years of its existence as a church body have clearly demonstrated a lack of appetite for the theological categories of classical Christianity. It produces activists, not thinkers. Its Lutheran identity has become very porous.

A third type of Lutheranism includes chiefly the office managers who have a nose for where the money and levers of power happen to be. They have technical expertise that could be useful in any business enterprise, and it doesn't particularly matter which one. The ELCA is currently run by these bureaucrats who excel in loyalty to the party apparatus that pays their salaries, but are not motivated by theological convictions. They are not opposed to Lutheran orthodoxy; they just don't know what it is. If they happen to know a little theology and speak glibly on church matters, they might even become bishops. Understanding the doctrines of the Christian faith is not a prerequisite.

This book will perhaps be of little interest to those who reflect any of the three types of Lutheranism described above. The red thread that runs throughout this book is the conviction that the evangelical catholic understanding of the biblical-Christian faith is the most faithful interpretation of the Lutheran theological heritage in an ecumenical age. The theological memoirs I wrote tell the story of how a child of Norwegian American pietism became a Lutheran with an evangelical catholic perspective (*Because of Christ: Memoirs of a Lutheran Theologian* [Eerdmans, 2010]). One conviction that evangelical catholics share is this: dogma is more important than denomination. Evangelical catholics tend to feel theologically more in harmony with each other, whatever their denominational affiliation, than with most of the theologians in their own church body. They enjoy a great sense of church unity and fellowship in Christ, because their theological thought moves within the framework of classical Christian orthodoxy. This was defined by the ancient councils and creeds of the church — Nicaea, Constantinople, Ephesus, and Chalcedon — all together handing down to us a theology that is christocentric, trinitarian, and monotheistic. It is a lamentable fact that the teaching theologians in the mainline Protestant seminaries, including some Lutheran, do not necessarily take seriously the great catholic and orthodox doctrines of the Christian faith. If they did, they would not have capitulated to the revisionist heterodoxy of radical theological feminism.

Some Lutheran theologians have attempted to organize the whole of theology around the doctrine of justification by faith alone. I think that is an abuse of the doctrine, even though I am fully committed to its use as an indispensable criterion for constructing the doctrine of salvation — soteriology. I am also greatly in favor of its hermeneutical function in biblical interpretation and its homiletical value in sermon preparation. I became convinced of this mostly by reading Luther's commentaries and sermons. However, I believe it would be wrong to try to derive the whole of Christian doctrine from this one article. Martin Kähler was one Lutheran theologian who attempted to do so. In so many ways he was on the right track. Before Albert Schweitzer wrote his book on the quest of the historical Jesus, Kähler had already declared that project of historical critical scholarship to be a dead-end and completely irrelevant to Christian faith. He was largely supported later in that respect by Paul Tillich, Karl Barth, and Emil Brunner. The modern quest of the historical Jesus was judged by them to be historically a failure and theologically of no significance.

Yet, it was Martin Kähler who structured his systematic theology by the article of justification by faith. His system was divided into three parts: 1) Christian Apologetics, concerning the presuppositions of justifying faith; 2) Evangelical Dogmatics, concerning the object of justifying faith; 3) Theological Ethics, concerning the manifestation of justifying faith. On his deathbed Kähler made the request that the *articulis stantis et cadentis ecclesiae* be inscribed on his gravestone. I could hardly wish better than to do the same. Gerhard Ebeling attempted a similar reduction of Christian doctrine by making the category of faith serve as the hub around which all the other articles of faith revolve.

Nevertheless, such an approach is impossible today in light of our knowledge of the origins of the Christian faith, the his-

14

tory of dogma, and the ecumenical dialogues with Roman Catholic and Eastern Orthodox theologians. In light of these factors we know that systematic theology that claims to be evangelical, catholic, and orthodox is based on the twin towers of Trinity and Christology. The article of justification by faith functions as a critical soteriological principle within this dogmatic framework and cannot by itself constitute it. That may sound like an unLutheran concession, but to require this one doctrine to be generative of all others is based on a mis-interpretation of the Lutheran Confessions, the *Book of Concord*. Lutheranism is not a self-authenticating movement within world Christianity. A Lutheran theology that would restrict itself to Luther's theology or the Lutheran Confessions would be an abrogation of their intention to serve as a reforming movement within western Christianity. I will elaborate on this point in the first chapter of this book, that deals with the question of Lutheran identity in an ecumenical age.

Chapter One
Lutheran Identity

I have been a Lutheran all my life, but not in the same church body. I was baptized in the Norwegian Lutheran Church in America (NLCA). In 1960 the ELC merged with the American Lutheran Church (ALC) to create The American Lutheran Church (TALC). Then I transferred my membership to the United Lutheran Church in America (ULCA) for professional reasons. In 1961 the ULCA became a part of the Lutheran Church in America (LCA) when it merged with three other church bodies — the Augustana Lutheran Church (Swedish), the American Evangelical Lutheran Church (Danish) and the Finnish Evangelical Lutheran Church. Then in 1987 all of the church bodies mentioned above formed a union to become the Evangelical Lutheran Church in America (ELCA), with the addition of the Association of Evangelical Lutheran Churches, the schismatic group that left the Lutheran Church–Missouri Synod.

Such an experience of the Lutheran alphabet soup in the United States has made clear to me that there is no such thing as the Lutheran Church, such as there is *the* Roman Catholic Church. The Roman Catholic Church is one church in that it is an organized society governed by the Pope and the Bishops in communion with him. There are many Lutheran churches both in the United States and the world. The majority of them belong to the Lutheran World Federation (LWF), a global communion of autonomous churches united by a common confession of faith based on the Holy Scriptures and expressed in the Ecumenical Creeds (Nicene, Chalcedonian, and Athanasian) and the Lutheran Confessions. The LWF now has 140 member churches in 79 countries, representing around 70 million Christians.

In 2017 Lutherans and Catholics from around the world will celebrate the 500th anniversary of Luther's nailing of his 95 theses to the door of the Castle Church in Wittenberg, Germany, the event that triggered the Reformation. In Luther's mind he was merely disputing the practice of selling certificates of indulgences to raise money to build St. Peter's Cathedral in Rome. He had no intention of founding a new church, let alone one named after him. Luther wrote, "I ask that no reference be made to my name; let them call themselves Christians, not Lutherans. After all, the teaching is not mine. Neither was I crucified for anyone. St. Paul in I Corinthians would not allow the Christians to call themselves Pauline or Petrine, but simply Christian. How then could I — poor stinking maggot-fodder that I am — come to have people call the children of Christ by my wretched name? Not so, my dear friends; let us abolish all party names and call ourselves Christians, after him whose teaching we hold." But that wasn't to be. Luther's name stuck. The "Lutheran" label was first used by Luther's Catholic opponents as a sobriquet to indicate the purely human origin of the Lutheran movement, thus disparaging the cause of the Reformation. That Lutheranism was nothing but a man-made religion was an element of Roman Catholic apologetics until the Second Vatican Council.

Luther's reform movement was too conservative for other Protestant reformers, in particular John Calvin, Huldreich Zwingli, and Thomas Müntzer. The followers of Martin Luther retained the core elements of the Catholic tradition, specifically the canonical Scriptures, the ancient Creeds, the liturgical rites, the sacraments of Baptism, Absolution, and the Lord's Supper, and an ordained clergy. Yet, contrary to the intent of Luther and Philip Melanchthon, his right-hand man, their reforming movement led to a schism that has kept the Western branch of Christianity divided for almost half a millennium.

New church structures, at first intended as interim arrangements until unity could be restored, eventually became permanently established to keep the Lutheran movement separated from its mother church.

Lutheranism spread from Germany, its birth place, to the Nordic countries — Denmark, Sweden, Norway, Iceland, and Finland — and it became their state religion. In Eastern Europe Lutheranism took shape as minority churches that often suffered persecution by the Catholic majority. Lutheranism reached America already in the 17th century, but it was not until the mass migrations between 1870 and 1920 that millions of Lutherans left Europe for the new country. The 19th century missionary movement planted new churches throughout Africa, Asia, and Latin America, making Lutheranism a global network of church bodies. Today the number of Lutherans in the world is around seventy million adherents.

Historically Lutheranism has been shaped by its understanding of the biblical message (the gospel) articulated in its classical confessions, the *Book of Concord*. From the start it had to define itself in relation to four major challenges to its identity: Roman Catholicism (Council of Trent), humanistic criticism (Erasmus of Rotterdam), Anabaptism (Thomas Müntzer), and the Swiss Reformation (Huldreich Zwingli and John Calvin). The history of Lutheran self-definition continued in the centuries that followed. It was characterized by fierce polemics between Orthodoxy that stressed pure doctrine, Pietism that called for a born-again experience, and the Enlightenment that applied rationalistic criticism to religion.

Such different expressions of the Lutheran heritage give rise to the question whether there are essentials that have persisted through changing times? Lutheranism began in the mind and soul of a friar who taught the Bible in an Augustinian monastery in the city of Wittenberg. It has been said so often, it's about time that Lutherans start believing it: Luther did not set out to start a new church. His focus was not on substituting his church for the one in which he was baptized, confirmed, and ordained. He was a Catholic until he was excommunicated, and when he was forced into exile. He remained a Catholic in exile until the day he died. Luther's chief concern has left its stamp on the movement that followed in his footsteps and came to be known in world history by his name.

As professor of Bible at the University of Wittenberg Luther gave lectures on the Psalms, Romans, Galatians, and Hebrews. In his commentaries he articulated an understanding of the gospel that later Lutheranism framed by three slogans — *sola gratia, sola fide,* and *sola scriptura. Sola gratia* — by grace alone — means that a person receives the gift of salvation solely by the sovereign will of God, without any cooperation from the human side (synergism). *Sola fide* — faith alone — means that a person becomes righteous in the sight of God solely through an act of trust in Christ apart from the works of the law. *Sola scriptura* — Scripture alone — means that the Old and New Testaments are the final standard by which all church teaching must be judged. The core of these *solas* may be summed up in one phrase — *solus Christus.* Jesus Christ is the sole basis of the Christian hope of salvation.

The Fox and the Hedgehog

A Greek poet by the name of Archilochus (7th century B.C.) is credited with this saying: "The fox knows many things, but the hedgehog knows one big thing." Lutherans are more like the hedgehog than the fox. They know one big thing, and that one thing is the gospel. This is the strength of Lutheranism, but it may also at times become its Achilles' heel. As we suggested in our preface, that can happen when everything in Christianity is reduced to a single principle — the article of justification by faith alone — as though all other doctrines, traditions, or structures are derivative or worse, mere matters of indifference (*adiaphora*). However, that does not negate the fact that no other church tradition has made concern for the purity of the gospel so central in its self-understanding. This is by no means an historical accident, since Lutheranism has been radically dependent on Luther and his determination to measure everything by the gospel. When building a house, it is important to have an accurate measuring stick. The gospel of justification by faith alone is the Lutheran measuring stick, but it is not the house.

As Lutherans today we should exercise a degree of humility by reminding ourselves that in making the article of justification our one big thing, we have thereby let Luther's personal religious experience shape our Lutheran identity in a way that makes us vulnerable to criticism by those who are not and have no interest in becoming Lutheran. If you saw the Luther film, you will recall how he became a monk (or friar). When scared to death by a thunderstorm, he cried out, "Help, St. Anna, and I will become a monk." So he did, and his troubles became serious. He was plagued by a guilty conscience and attacks of depression. He called them "*Anfechtungen*," a German word for his intense spiritual trials, perhaps including the fear of damnation. Luther went to his father confessor, Dr. Staupitz, and asked, "How can I find a gracious God? All I see in my fasting and prayers is the face of a wrathful God." No sooner did he get absolved of one sin, and another one popped up to torment him, driving him into deeper despair. Dr. Staupitz told Luther to study for a doctorate in theology and major in biblical studies. Had Luther not done that, there would have been no Reformation.

When Luther dug deeply into the Scriptures, he stumbled upon a verse in St. Paul's *Epistle to the Romans:* "The one who is righteous will live by faith." The verse contains not a single word about the law or the works that the law demands. As important as they are, they are not the means by which God addresses us with words of his love. Christ alone is the messenger of God's love. A "happy exchange" (*fröhliche Wechsel*) takes place through faith in Christ. He gives us his righteousness in exchange for our sinfulness. Christ became sin for us that that we might be clothed in his righteousness. To be sure, God requires righteousness, but the gospel says that he gives what he demands. No longer did Luther believe

21

that he had to do enough good works to tip the scales of God's justice in his favor. No longer was salvation from sin and guilt a process of cooperation between God's grace and human effort.

But what blew the cork out of the bottle was precisely the priestly malpractice of selling salvation, through the sale of coupons or certificates of indulgence, which a person could buy for himself or for friends and relatives squirming in purgatory with the pain of punishment for sins committed before they died. John Tetzel was the fiery preacher who chanted the slogan: "As soon as the coin in the coffer rings, the soul from purgatory springs." The money gained was sent to Rome to help build St. Peter's Cathedral. That got the Pope involved and made Luther, good German that he was, mightily disturbed. The ensuing struggle eventually implicated the highest authorities in the empire — papacy, the princes, and the emperor himself. Despite efforts to silence Luther and to kill him, the fight ended in a stalemate at the Peace of Augsburg in 1555. The emperor could not defeat the princes who protected Luther. The Lutheran churches became territorial churches and the princes became emergency bishops, ruling not only in secular things in society, but also in spiritual matters within the church.

We have had to delve into a little bit of history because as heirs of the Lutheran Reformation, we are endowed with the Lutheran DNA, including good and bad genes, strengths and weaknesses. The one big thing for Lutherans — teaching the doctrine of justification through faith alone — has come down to us from Luther's spiritual encounter with his conscience and the Bible. Luther felt assaulted by the demons of sin, death, anxiety, guilt, wrath, and fear, all these soul-destroying works of the devil. Now what if later Lutherans did not share the same sort of negative experiences or at least not to the same degree? Would the doctrine of justification through faith alone apart from the works of the law enjoy the same premier status?

Luther's closest colleague was Philip Melanchthon. He was not nearly such a troubled soul. Luther came at things with a sledge hammer and a fiery temperament; Melanchthon was noted for his soft touch and irenic spirit. The generation of Lutherans who followed them split into two factions, threatening the unity of Lutheranism. Toward the end of his life Luther often wondered whether his entire reforming effort might not have been in vain. The theologians who considered themselves true followers of Luther were called "gnesio-Lutherans." The other faction was called Philippism, because this group of theologians remained closer to Philip Melanchthon's outlook. So they went at it, tooth and nail, theologians at each others' throats like rabid dogs. Melanchthon prayed to God that they might be spared what he called the "fury of theologians" (*rabies theologorum*).

It is good for contemporary Lutherans to be reminded that their confessional theology was hammered out on the anvil of intense controversy, with many issues at stake. Here are some of the questions they disputed (*quaestiones disputatae*).

1. Original sin. How much damage did the sin of Adam and Eve do to human nature? Did sin bring about a total corruption of every human faculty, or did it leave only a smudge, a stain, a defect — leaving some good in human beings?

2. Free will. Luther taught that the will is in bondage and cannot free itself in matters pertaining to salvation. However, some other Lutherans thought that was too extreme — some vestige of freedom remains after the fall so that persons are free to accept or reject God's offer of salvation.

3. Sanctification. Theologians debated whether salvation is a two-step process, justification understood as the starting point and sanctification as the ongoing process of growth in grace.

4. Good works. Theologians debated whether good works are necessary for salvation or rather harmful for salvation, inasmuch as the Old Adam that remains after conversion may put its trust in them, and not rely solely on the grace of Christ.

5. Law and gospel. Theologians argued about the proper distinction between law and gospel. The law demands and accuses, but does not the preaching of the gospel do that too? Is the gospel not also a proclamation unto repentance and not

exclusively a proclamation of forgiveness? Should the functions of the law and the gospel be so completely separated and set in contrast to each other?

6. The Third Use of the Law. The *Formula of Concord* describes three uses of the law. The first is the political use of the law. We must stop at the stop sign; it's the law of the State and it applies to everyone. The second use of the law is accusatory; it shows the sins and wrongdoings of people, driving them to repentance and in search of mercy. Is there a third use of the law that applies to Christians after their conversion? Orthodox Lutherans said, yes, because Christians, no matter how advanced in sanctification, need the guidelines and admonitions of the law.

7. Predestination and Election. The question here is whether God elects those whom he foresees will choose to believe in Christ by their own free will, or whether faith is the work of the Holy Spirit, something God predestines and elects to accomplish before an individual has any choice in the matter. Jesus said, "You did not choose me, but I chose you."[1] The apostle Paul writes, "And those whom God predestined he also called; and those whom he called, he also justified; and those whom he justified he also glorified."[2] The way of salvation is from beginning to end the work of God the Holy Spirit. The Lutherans unanimously rejected John Calvin's idea of double predestination, according to which God predestinates some to be saved and some to be damned. Lutheran theologians asserted that such a view is a flat-out denial of the biblical verse, "God our Savior ... desires everyone to be saved and to come to the knowledge of the truth."[3]

The Lutherans got their heavyweight theologians together and produced the *Formula of Concord* — which they signed. This meant that the Lutheran movement would remain unified in face of great opposition from the Romans on the right and the Protestants on the left. Before too long, however, the arguments did not go away. They erupted again when the Lutheran Pietists dismissed the *Formula of Concord*. Lutheran

Pietists did not approve of what seemed to them hair-splitting distinctions of the scholastic dogmaticians who had been schooled in Aristotelian logic.

It is ironic that the very tradition that has affirmed the doctrine of justification by faith as the article by which the church stands or falls has been devoid of harmony concerning its proper interpretation. What is the point of trumpeting this doctrine as the chief article, if Lutherans cannot agree on what it means? It runs the risk of becoming an empty slogan. The problem area lies in how theologians understand the relationship between faith and justification. If faith alone justifies a sinner before God, that is, gains forgiveness of sins and puts a person in a right relationship with God, the all-important question becomes: "How does a person get such saving faith?" To answer the question theologians had to move away from justification to regeneration. Regeneration means "born again." Only a regenerated person can have faith. In spelling out the way of salvation, the seventeenth century Lutheran dogmaticians placed regeneration prior to justification, to explain how a person comes to repentance and faith, that is, how a person attains the subjective condition of faith required for God to justify a sinner.

This way of thinking is a departure from Luther's teaching. The precise relation between faith and justification has been a murky area in Lutheran dogmatic teaching. The problem is that while Lutherans taught that sinners are justified by faith apart from the works of the law, they run the risk of turning faith into a work that a person must somehow perform by an exercise of the mind, together with an act of the will and a decision of trust in the mercy of Christ. Faith was defined by the dogmaticians to consist of three parts: knowledge (*notitia*), assent (*assensus*), and trust (*fiducia*). Next question -- how much knowledge, how firm the assent, and how pure the trust will be required? Will memorizing Luther's *Small Catechism* suffice? The doctrine that was supposed to unite Lutherans ran the danger of "dying the death of a thousand qualifications" (Antony Flew).

For Luther justification meant the forgiveness of sins. For-giveness of sins is preached as an objective gift of God to sin-ners, on account of Christ, not because they *already* repent and believe, but in order that they might do so. Bringing that condition about is the work of the Holy Spirit. Faith is a gift of the Holy Spirit, not a work which humans are able to perform by their own "reason and strength." This is what Luther said in the *Small Catechism:* "I believe that I cannot by my own rea-son or strength believe in Jesus Christ, my Lord, or come to him; but instead the Holy Spirit has called me by the Gospel, enlightened me with his gifts, sanctified and kept me in the true faith, even as he calls, gathers, enlightens, and sanctifies the whole Christian Church on earth and keeps it with Jesus Christ in the one true faith."

The Helsinki Fiasco

In 1963 Lutherans from around the world met in Helsinki, Finland, under the auspices of the Lutheran World Federa-tion. The chief item on the agenda was to produce a consen-sus statement on the doctrine of justification that would re-solve long-standing misinterpretations and disagreements. If this doctrine is the one big thing for Lutherans, it would seem important for Lutherans to present a united front to the rest of the Christian world. Otherwise, Lutherans in conversation with other Christian denominations would present an ambiguous witness. And that is exactly what happened.

The outcome of the meeting in Helsinki was that time ran out before the delegates could draft and vote on a consensus statement. The Germans and Scandinavians and Americans could not agree. At least three positions, maybe more, were in play. First, the confessional Lutherans wanted to draft a docu-ment based on the *Book of Concord* that all could subscribe. Second, those coming from the tradition of Lutheran Pietism felt no allegiance to the *Book of Concord* and held a more common-sense psychological account of the way of salvation (*ordo salutis*). Third, there was new input from the existentialist theologians who sought a new idiom and new language that supposedly modern people could better understand. Modern people are not likely to have read the old dogmaticians and are inclined to say, "a plague on both your houses," to the orthodox and the pietists.

To complicate things even further, we now have the new Finnish interpretation of Luther's theology[4] that links the idea of the righteousness of God with the Russian Orthodox concept of *theosis*, meaning, divinization. In dialogue with the Russian Orthodox theologians the Finnish theologians learned that their Orthodox partners did not understand the doctrine of justification, and even after explaining it to them, the Russians said, "Nyet!" The doctrine of justification by faith has scarcely any resonance in the writings of the Eastern Fathers. So the Finnish theologians in dialogue claim to have discovered in Luther's writings a point of contact in the idea of *theosis*. This novel interpretation remains very much a matter in dispute among Luther scholars. The LWF meeting in Helsinki ended without an agreement. This is why I have referred to it as the "Helsinki fiasco."

The Election Controversy

As one who was raised within the framework of Norwegian Lutheran Pietism I can vouch for the fact that the *Book of Concord* was not held in high esteem. Our touchstone, besides the Bible, was Luther's *Small Catechism*. When I entered Luther Seminary in St. Paul in 1952, the campus was aflame in controversy, spear-headed by two professors, both of Norwegian descent, one a pietist whose name was George Aus and the other orthodox whose name was Herman Preus. The old controversies that go back to the sixteenth century between the gnesio-Lutherans, followers of Luther, and the Phillipists, followers of Melanchthon, were now being re-played at Luther Seminary. I had taken many religion courses at St. Olaf College, majored in philosophy, and read a lot of Kierkegaard, but I was not prepared for the controversy I was about to encounter. On one of my first days on campus I saw a big huddle of boys on the sidewalk outside the library, obviously the scene of over-heated verbal exchanges. I stuck my head into the huddle to find out what was going on. One of the boys turned to me and asked, "Whose side are you on?" I didn't know know enough to answer one way or another. A short time later one of the upperclassmen gave me the lowdown. Aus believes this; Preus believes the opposite. And besides they don't like each other. They live next door to each other, but they don't converse.

Meanwhile the controversy was spreading beyond the seminary. Pastors and congregations of the Norwegian Lutheran Church in America were getting wind of it and beginning to take sides. This dispute threatened to be church-dividing. The president of the church, Johan A. Aasgaard, wrote a letter to all the pastors, reminding them that when three Norwegian Synods merged in 1917,[5] they dealt with the controversy on election and free will and, having reached no consensus, they had agreed to disagree. Both sides, the Pietists and the Orthodox, had pledged to co-exist within the NLCA.

The Joint Declaration on the Doctrine of Justification

To bring this discussion of the doctrine of justification up-to-date, we need to make mention of the remarkable event that took place October, 1999, on the eve of the new millenium, in Augsburg, Germany — the signing of the "Joint Declaration on the Doctrine of Justification" (JDDJ) by the Roman Catholic Church and the Lutheran World Federation. Thus, as it was reported at the time, they "consigned to oblivion" the mutual condemnations of the sixteenth century.[6] Since this deals with the one big thing that Lutherans hold dear, the agreement made a lot of pastors and theologians nervous. For one thing, it put a damper on celebrating the festival of the Reformation in the same old polemical way. If on that occasion we no longer feel free to trot out our familiar fighting slogans, wave our crusading banners, sing our chauvinistic rousers, thanking God that he has given to our church the gift of the pure preaching of the gospel, what then should we do? The spirit of ecumenism has changed all that. No longer should unbelievers be able to scoff at Christians: "Look at those Christians, how they fight and hate each other, all in the name of Christ." Now, instead, the old condemnations are fading away. My suggestion to Lutherans is that on Reformation Day or Reformation Sunday Lutherans should invite Catholics to participate, perhaps even hold a joint service of thanksgiving to God for the new day of ecumenical conversation and cooperation, leading down the road to greater unity and shared communion.

Several hundred German Lutheran professors, together with a handful of Americans, signed a letter declaring their opposition to the JDDJ. Their point was that this declaration covers over some historic confessional differences between Lutherans and Catholics on the doctrine of justification. I believe they may be right about that, but we need to keep in mind that all consensus documents, including the Nicene and Chalcedonian Creeds, aim to find common ground that both opposing sides share, rather than reiterate the traditional points of disagreement. In any case, according to the JDDJ Lutherans and Catholics confess together certain basic truths:

1) that all persons depend completely on the saving grace of God for their salvation;

2) that God forgives sin by grace and at the same time frees human beings from sin's enslaving power and imparts the gift of new life in Christ;

3) that sinners are justified by faith in the saving action of God in Christ;

4) that in baptism the Holy Spirit unites one with Christ, justifies, and truly renews the person;

5) that persons are justified by faith in the gospel "apart from works prescribed by the law";

6) that the faithful can rely on the mercy and promises of God;

7) that good works — a Christian life lived in faith, hope and love — follow justification and are its fruits.

Then the Joint Declaration states that "a consensus in basic truths of the doctrine of justification now exists between Lutherans and Catholics." It goes on to declare that the mutual condemnations of the sixteenth century no longer apply to the teachings of the other church. It concludes with this prayer:

> We give thanks to the Lord for this decisive step forward on the way to overcoming the division of the church. We ask the Holy Spirit to lead us further toward that visible unity which is Christ's will.

It seems to me disingenuous for Lutheran theologians to be overly critical of the JDDJ when their own church bodies could reach no consensus at the LWF Assembly in Helsinki. This agreement between Lutherans and Catholics is possibly as far-reaching as any agreement that world Lutherans could reach amongst themselves. In my view the JDDJ is a miracle of divine grace. There is nothing of its kind in the last 500 years. However, this does not mean that the Roman Catholic Church is yet prepared to lift the ban of welcoming Lutherans to the same Table of the Lord. We Lutherans can welcome Catholics, but Catholics do not yet see their way to welcome others than Roman Catholics in good standing. Closed communion is an ecclesial scandal, a practice that has insufficient theological warrant from Scripture. If Christians and Churches that have been divided for generations can come together and greet each other as brothers and sisters in Christ and actually confess that they all belong to Christ, then who among them has the authority or audacity to divide those whom Christ calls into his fellowship of grace?

Now, if the doctrine of justification is the one big thing for Lutherans, then according to this document a person may become a Roman Catholic, join the Roman Catholic Church, without having to renounce his or her Lutheran beliefs. That is exactly what some Lutherans, for example, Richard John

Neuhaus, have said when they entered into the Roman Communion. My rejoinder is that signing the JDDJ is a necessary step but still insufficient, because the big elephant in the room remains standing, and that is the dogma of papal infallibility and the papal claim to universal jurisdiction. The dogma of papal infallibility was not adopted by the Roman Catholic Church until the latter part of the nineteenth century, at the First Vatican Council. This Council declared that when the Pope speaks *ex cathedra*, he has a God-given authority to make definitions regarding the doctrines of the faith that are infallible and immutable of themselves (*ex sese*), without requiring the consent of the church.

Types of Lutheranism

With the rise of the ecumenical movement after the Second Vatican Council in the 1960s, Lutheranism has been a movement in search of its ecclesial and theological identity. Lutheranism oscillates worldwide between a centrifugal force that brings about ever more variegated expressions, on the one hand, and a centripetal force that aims to seek common ground and greater unity, on the other hand. The diversity among Lutherans is more readily visible than unity. I will use the typological method to show the varieties of Lutheranism in history and today in order to radicalize the question of its identity and future.

Lutheran Scholasticism

After numerous theological disputes Lutheran theologians in the sixteenth century produced a book of confessions that spelled out their agreements, contained in *The Book of Concord* (1580).[7] Subsequently Lutheran theologians, Martin Chemnitz among them, adopted the *loci* method that Philip Melanchthon used in writing his *Loci Communes Theologici* (1521) to present a summary of Christian doctrine. During the seventeenth century Lutheran dogmaticians replaced the *loci* method with the scholastic method that was practiced in the universities, due to the revival of Aristotle's philosophy. They used philosophical terms and syllogistic reasoning to interpret the Christian faith and to defend the orthodoxy of *The Book of Concord.* In the nineteenth century Heinrich Schmid compiled a textbook of theological statements from the writings of the sixteenth and seventeenth century Lutheran theologians representing Lutheran scholasticism.[8] Regrettably these documents of classical Lutheranism are scarcely read and studied by contemporary Lutheran theologians. Yet, this type of Lutheran theology prevailed until the rise of rationalism in the period of the Enlightenment and the attacks of Pietism on what it called "dead orthodoxy."

Every succeeding generation of Lutheran theologians should feel obligated to measure itself with reference to the source documents of classical Lutheran orthodoxy. While this is necessary, it is not sufficient. A mere repristination of seventeenth century scholasticism will not equip Lutherans today to deal with the issues that the church must face in every new situation. Their struggles of today are not necessarily the same as those of a half millennium ago. The seventeenth century Lutheran dogmaticians were fighting Jesuits, Calvinists, and Anabaptists, all challenges from within Christendom. We are living in a post-Christendom age that requires a fresh reading of Scripture and a return to the ante-Nicene Fathers who lived and taught in a missionary situation before Emperor Constantine declared Christianity to be the official religion of the empire.

Lutheran Pietism

Pietism was a renewal movement within Lutheranism in the seventeenth-eighteenth centuries. It was re-awakened in the nineteenth century throughout Europe and North America. Philip Jakob Spener (1635-1705) has been called "the father of pietism." He was the author of its classic manifesto, *Pia Desideria,* a clarion call for a reform of Lutheranism. Lutheran orthodoxy, he believed, had become ossified by an over-zealous concern for pure doctrine at the expense of personal piety and holy living. Pietism spread by meeting in houses for Bible study and prayer apart from the organized church. These meetings were called "little churches within the church" (*ecclesiolae in ecclesia*). Pietism became known for the following emphases: a devotional, rather than a doctrinal, approach to the study of the Bible; leadership in the hands of the laity rather than the clergy; the necessity of a regenerative experience rather than relying on the formality of infant baptism; a separation of Christians from the world and a strict code of morality (no dancing, no drinking, no smoking, no card playing, etc.).

Many orthodox Lutheran theologians and pastors took exception to what they deemed the excesses of pietism. Critics of the pietist movement asserted that its conception of Christianity bred individualism, subjectivism, and legalism. Its strategy for reform leads away from the church as a body of believers, the rites of public worship, and the sacraments instituted by Christ. By stressing piety over doctrine, it led to unionistic movements that de-emphasize the importance of classical church teachings, as formulated in the ancient Creeds of the Church and the Lutheran Confessions. The result is that the children and grandchildren of the pietists often became liberals, because the category of experience — the cardinal principle of pietism — cannot of itself generate structures faithful to the Holy Scriptures and the creedal teachings of orthodox Christianity.

The Evangelical Protestants of today are the heirs of both Lutheran and Reformed pietistic movements of the nineteenth century. They are in earnest pursuit of their identity. One wing is trying to reconnect with the Great Tradition of pre-Reformation Christianity, and another wing is moving in the opposite direction of opening itself to modern modes of thought and societal challenges.[9] When pietism lost the church as its medium, its offspring became unsure of where to go, whether back to the sources of classical Christianity or more deeply into modes of contemporary culture. The instability of pietism as a type of Christianity is due to its alienation from church tradition and its reliance on the ephemeral oscillations of feelings and experiences.

Lutheran Liberalism

The eighteenth century Enlightenment was a watershed in the history of Lutheran theology. The Enlightenment established reason as the chief source and ultimate criterion of religious knowledge and scientific truth. This placed in question all texts and traditions that claim to be founded on the authority of the Bible and church teachings. The faith and morals of historic Christianity had to be subjected to the litmus test of modern scientific views of nature and history. The newly developed methods of historical research had to be applied not only to the Old Testament and its account of creation and the history of Israel, but also to the New Testament and its story of Jesus and the origin of the church.

The rationalistic point of view aims to pervade every endeavor in Christian theology and biblical interpretation. Nothing should remain the same this side of the Enlightenment. To say it in colloquial terms, everything is up for grabs. The view of Lutheran orthodoxy that the Christian faith is based on God's unique and supreme revelation recorded in the Holy Scriptures and rightly interpreted in the Creeds and Confessions of the church underwent a gradual process of disintegration.

Some theologians used the philosophical categories of Immanuel Kant to elaborate the truths of Christianity. It was Kant who asked and answered the question, "What is Enlightenment?" (*Was ist Aufklärung?*) Others built their systems in reliance on the idealistic philosophy of Georg Wilhelm Friedrich Hegel. Still others looked to Friedrich Schleiermacher, known as the father of modern Protestant theology. The old question that Tertullian asked, "What does Athens have to do with Jerusalem?" was answered by liberal Lutheran theologians by putting Athens in the driver's seat. The same story was played out in the twentieth century, no longer predominantly with the thought categories of Kant, Hegel, or Schleiermacher, but with those of Alfred North Whitehead, Martin Heidegger, or Ludwig Wittgenstein. The ancient sources of Scripture and church tradition were out-balanced

34

by modern appeals to reason and experience, and the latter hold the place of preeminence as sources and criteria of truth.

Lutheran Catholicism

This is a label for a fourth type of Lutheran conviction and theology. Evangelical catholics share a vision of the church that exists in historical and spiritual continuity with the apostolic church founded by Jesus and the apostles and that continued through ancient and medieval times up to the sixteenth century Reformation. Continuity is the important concept. Evangelical catholics believe that modern Protestantism prides itself in breaking away from institutions and sacraments that provide continuity. Especially in an ecumenical age evangelical catholics tend to draw from the traditions they share with the Roman Catholic and Orthodox Churches. They maintain that the traditions of the first millennium of Christianity are not the exclusive capital of Roman Catholics and the Orthodox. Nathan Söderblom (1866-1931), archbishop of Sweden, stated that there are three main blocs of world Christianity -- Greek Catholic, Roman Catholic, and Evangelical Catholic.

Evangelical catholics cannot say it often enough: Luther had no desire to create a new church, least of all one named after him. "Evangelical" and "catholic" are not contradictory terms. When Luther instituted some evangelical reforms, he did not cease to be catholic. Evangelical catholics generally call for the restoration of episcopacy in apostolic succession, the celebration of Holy Communion as the central act of Christian worship, the return of private confession, the use of a rich array of liturgical forms, as well as the establishment of religious societies, and in a few cases, even monasteries. In our day "The Society of the Holy Trinity" (founded in the United States, September 1997) is a splendid example of the liturgical and sacramental commitments common to evangelical catholics.

Lutheran Confessionalism

There are some Lutherans who will not identify themselves with any of the four types we have described. They do not merely repristinate seventeenth century Lutheran scholasticism, nor are they beholden to pietistic biblicism or liberal Protestantism, and most certainly they are not evangelical catholics. They may have some affinity with one or another of these types of Lutheranism, but their agenda is quite other. They think of themselves as confessional Lutherans.

After World War II the Lutheran World Federation was founded to bring autonomous Lutheran churches together, but it had no ecclesiological significance. A federation is not a church. Lutheran unity was on the mind of church leaders around the world. It was a unity based on a common confession of faith, underscoring the original intent of Lutheranism not to produce a new church but to be a reforming movement for the sake of the one, holy, catholic church to which they belonged. The reason that no article concerning the church appears in the Lutheran Confessions is that the authors took the reality of the church of which they were members for granted.

The latter half of the twentieth century witnessed a renaissance of confessional Lutheran theology in Europe and the United States. We have only to recall the contributions of Gustaf Aulén and Anders Nygren in Sweden, Regin Prenter and K. E. Skydsgaard in Denmark, Lennart Pinomaa and Tuomo Mannermaa in Finland, Edmund Schlink and Peter Brunner in Germany in order to appreciate the power and scope of Lutheran theology during the latter half of the twentieth century. A chief impetus was, of course, the outpouring of books on Luther and the Reformation by both Protestant and Catholic scholars. The ecumenical movement also provided the occasion for Lutherans to bring their strongest theological traditions into dialogue with other churches, Roman Catholic, Orthodox, and Protestant. It was theological concern for the doctrines of the faith, and especially the article of justification, that Lutherans brought to the ecumenical roundtable.

A survey of all the dialogues over the past fifty years shows that ecclesiology has not been the strong suit of Lutheranism. In fact it has been something of an embarrassment. The five types of Lutheranism we have identified embody essentially very different and even contradictory concepts of the church, and there is no sign that anything like a coherent unified understanding is emerging in world Lutheranism.[10] This is not by accident. Such diversity is inherent in the schismatic situation in which Lutheranism actually found itself as a theological reforming movement for the sake of the western branch of Christianity. The adherents of the Lutheran Reformation have had no choice but to express themselves improvisationally through a myriad of *ad hoc* institutional arrangements to care for the preaching of the Word and the administration of the sacraments within assemblies of believers who gather for worship and service in the name of Jesus Christ.

We have described five types of Lutheranism. In real life seldom does a single type do justice to any theologian or church body. Most of us are hybrids and somewhat eclectic, mixing and matching elements from more than one type.

New Interpretations of the Gospel in Contemporary Theology

Lutheran theology was born in a university and ever since Lutherans have been in the vanguard of creative theological scholarship in the areas of Scripture, history of doctrine, and systematic theology. I have devoted the last 50 years of my life to attend to that tradition as best I can.[11] I am a Lutheran by conviction, more like the hedgehog than the fox. In Luke's story of Mary and Martha, Jesus said to Martha, "Martha, Martha, you are worried and distracted by many things; there is need of only one thing. Mary has chosen the better part, which will not be taken away from her."[12] That's the difference between the fox and the hedgehog.

After a century of liberal Protestant theology from Friedrich Schleiermacher to Albrecht Ritschl and Adolf von Harnack, Karl Barth gave new impetus to a theology focussed on the Word of God in continuity with the sixteenth century Reformation. He became famous overnight for his Commentary on Paul's *Epistle to the Romans*. He criticized modern Protestant theology for being anthropocentric. Such a theology focusses on what humans think about God based on their own reason and experience. Real theology is based on what God has revealed, written down in Holy Scripture and transmitted in the Christian tradition. Theology should be theocentric, Barth said. And he was joined in this basic conviction by like-minded theologians such as Emil Brunner, Eduard Thurneysen, Dietrich Bonhoeffer, Friedrich Gogarten, Otto Weber, Thomas Torrance and others, all of whom contributed in various ways to establish what has been called neo-orthodox theology. I learned from all these great minds, but there were others who exercised an even greater influence in shaping my understanding of specifically Lutheran theology. I have always had the greatest respect and appreciation for Karl Barth, ever since reading his *Commentary on Paul's Epistle to the Romans*. That was an unforgettable religious experience. But Barth is no Lutheran, so I have never considered myself a card-carrying Barthian. Barth stands more in the tradition of the Swiss Refomers, John Calvin and Huldreich Zwingli, than in that of Martin Luther and Philip Melanchthon.

The Lutherans who have had the greatest influence on the shape and content of my theological thought are Paul J. Tillich (1886-1965), Anders Nygren (1890-1978), Gustaf Aulén (1879-1977), Edmund Schlink (1903-1984), Wolfhart Pannenberg (1928-), George Lindbeck (1923-), and Robert W. Jenson (1930-). There are only two Americans on that list, and the latter happens to be my best friend. I cannot think of any other American Lutheran theologians to whom I am as greatly indebted as to those on that list of names. I am going to identify only one or two concepts or motifs from each of these theologians that have made a significant impact on my mind.

Paul Tillich's favorite word was ontology. What does that have to do with the gospel? The word is not in the Bible; it comes from Greek philosophy. Ontology is the study of being. Tillich applied his ontological thinking to anthropology and emphasized that the human predicament is profoundly ontological. Humans are distorted in the depths of their being. Sin is ontological, not merely psychological. So the remedy must be ontological, and that remedy is the New Being that appeared in Jesus as the Christ. One other thing I learned from Tillich, and that is what he called the "method of correlation." The idea is simple; there is no point in answering questions that are not asked. A cogent answer must correlate to the question. The Christian gospel is the answer to the question of human existence. In terms of preaching, this means that a sermon should convey a message from God that relates to the common human condition. The function of the law is to disclose what's wrong, and the function of the gospel is to tell what God has done to make things right. That should make sense to a preacher of the Word of God.

Anders Nygren's major work was *Agapé and Eros*. He contrasted the biblical idea of God's *agapeic* love with other kinds of love: *eros* (Plato's idea of aesthetic love), *philia* (Aristotle's idea of friendship love), and *libido* (Freud's idea of sexual love). *Agapé* is God's condescending love acted out in Jesus' life, death, and resurrection. God loves us not because we are so lovable, but in spite of our rebellion and waywardness. Nygren contrasted *agapé*, the fundamental Christian motif, with *nomos*, the fundamental Jewish motif, and with *eros*, the fundamental Greek-Hellenistic motif. Thus, he called his method "motif research."

Gustaf Aulén wrote many books, but the one that influenced my thinking the most is *Christus Victor, An Historical Study of the Three Main Types of the Idea of Atonement*. The doctrine of atonement is the interpretation of the suffering and death of Jesus on the cross. The *Christus Victor* motif takes off from what Paul wrote in II Cor. 5: 19: "God was in Christ reconciling the world to himself." That includes all things — all things in heaven, all things on earth, all nations, and all human beings. All who live under the tyranny of the powers of sin, death, wrath, fear, and the devil have been reconciled to God for Christ's sake. The gospel does not settle for a slice of the world, but encompasses the totality of reality. There is a universalism of the gospel that is not heretical. Many are so afraid of the wrong kind of universalism that they have abandoned the right kind that Paul intended with the *ta panta* passages (I Cor. 15: 28; Eph. 1:23; Col. 3:11).

Edmund Schlink was my teacher at the University of Heidelberg. I chose to go to Heidelberg because it had the best theological faculty at the time, especially for someone who wanted to learn how to become a Lutheran systematic theologian. Edmund Schlink was the author of *Theology of the Lutheran Confessions*, a book he wrote as a prolegomena to Christian dogmatics. Schlink's kind of confessional Lutheranism became a model for me, for several reasons. First, he understood the creeds and confessions of the church as faithful expositions of Holy Scripture. They are not a second source of divine revelation, but interpretations of what the Bible says under new historical circumstances. Second, the distinction between law and gospel is the key hermeneutical principle of the Lutheran Confessions. That has stuck with me. Third, the Confessions are radically christocentric — they point to Christ. Fourth, the Lutheran Confessions are not intended to serve as the constitution of a new independent church body, but as the ecumenical consensus of the faith confessed by the one holy, catholic church through the centuries. In his latter years, inspired by his experience as an official observer at the Second Vatican Council, Schlink went on to write a huge tome entitled, *Ecumenical Dogmatics*. It is the manifesto of an evangelical catholic theologian.

Wolfhart Pannenberg was a student of Edmund Schlink and received his doctorate from the University of Heidelberg. I first met him when I was a student in Heidelberg, 1957-1958. He was already teaching as what they called a *Privat-Docent*. At that time Protestant theology was polarized between the Barthians and the Bultmannians. To the credit of Pannenberg, he inaugurated a new approach that went beyond Barth and Bultmann. Barth was favored by conservatives and Bultmann by liberals. My basic intuition was that I belonged to neither camp, but I could learn from both. Pannenberg overcame the impasse with his idea of "revelation as history."[13] Both Barth and Bultmann were widely accused of not doing justice to the study of history because it had been taken captive by historical positivism. Pannenberg said, revelation does not happen *in* history or *above* history but as history, that is, in and through real historical events that can be attested by ear and eye-witnesses. The test case is the resurrection of Jesus. Did Jesus really rise from the dead? Was the resurrection a real historical event? Pannenberg answered, "Yes!" That was the breakthrough, because up to that point theologians tried to circumvent the idea of history when dealing with the resurrection of Jesus. But the resurrection is not only an historical event; it is an eschatological event. Thus, eschatology was reclaimed for theology, not as something above and beyond time, but as the future and final end of history that has already occurred proleptically in Jesus of Nazareth, in his life, death, and resurrection.

George Lindbeck is the son of a Lutheran missionary; that is something we have in common. His parents served in China, mine in Madagascar. This experience of growing up in the missionary situation helps to explain the ecumenical outlook that shapes both his thinking and mine. Ecumenism was born on the mission field. Many missionaries came to realize that their denominational identification was more an obstacle than a help in conveying the essence of the gospel. Their experience caused them to question whether the Christian divisions in the West and the North should continue to be replicated in the East and the South. Ecumenism was conceived as an emergency response to the scandal of church disunity. George Lindbeck was an observer at the Second Vatican Council. He has been the most important American Lutheran interpreter of its proceedings and statements. Much of my ecumenical thought is indebted to Lindbeck's pioneering proposals. Without any doubt he has been one of the most important ecumenical theologians in America.

Robert W. Jenson and I have been close companions and colleagues during our respective theological journeys of more than fifty years. To explain the measure of his influence on my thinking in particular as well as on contemporary systematic theology in general would merit more than a paragraph or two. Jenson's most important contribution has to do with the doctrine of the Trinity. He is one of a company of theologians who have reaffirmed the Trinity in new and creative ways: Wolfhart Pannenberg, Jürgen Moltmann, Thomas Torrance, John Zizioulas, Hans Urs von Balthasar, and Eberhard Jüngel. For one whole century the theology of liberal Protestantism in Germany — from Friedrich Schleiermacher and Albrecht Ritschl to Adolf von Harnack and Rudolf Bultmann — functioned with virtually no doctrine of the Trinity. Its doctrine of God was basically unitarian or modalistic and its Christology was Ebionitic or Arian. There was no real Trinity. Father, Son, and Holy Spirit were mere symbols of three ways to express how Christians claim they experience God. This means that the distinction between the three persons of the Trinity has no basis in the reality of God, but only in a psychology of religious experience.

I could go on to deal with what other contemporary theologians have contributed to a lively theology of the gospel for the church and its mission. The gospel has been and always is in a struggle to hold its own against countervailing movements that arise from modern culture, philosophy, and science. The task of a Christian theology is to serve as a defense attorney for his or her client, and the client in this case is the faith of the Christian church. A theologian's work is to be judged good or bad, depending on how well it serves the church and its gospel message.

On Tearing Down the Ladders to Heaven

It is because of its concentration on the gospel that Lutheran preaching at its best has been prophetically critical of intellectual arrogance, moralistic works-righteousness, and religious sentimentalism. It is in the nature of religion to construct ladders to heaven. It is in the nature of the gospel to tear them down. There are three stairways to heaven that Lutherans love to tear down. In doing this they model their actions on the Old Testament story of the Tower of Babel.

The first is the ladder of intellectualism. Intellectualism holds that one's relation to God is determined by one's knowledge of divine things. This might mean believing in doctrines that can be proved by reason alone or, failing that, at least guaranteed by an authority that is claimed to be infallible. The infallible authority could be the Pope or the Bible. Salvation is then understood as assent to a system of beliefs rather than a child-like trust in the gracious love of God in Jesus Christ. The intellectualist believes that to be saved everyone must hold the same correct ideas. This is the perennial danger of orthodoxy, love it as I do. A person is asked to place his or her trust in an external authority; it may be the authority of the Bible, the church, the creeds, the pope, or the democratic majority. The hedgehog is a spoilsport who thinks that no one can be saved by the works of one's intellect, not even if that means assent to the traditional doctrines of orthodox Christianity. Orthodoxy is great, but it is not the way of salvation. We are saved not by true doctrines. Although I work hard to understand and teach the true doctrines of the church, I do not place my trust in the most gnesio-Lutheran confessional theology I know. At the bottom line is this: we are not saved by the good works of our intellect, as important as they are.

Moralism is a second ladder. Moralism takes pride in obedience to ethical virtues, traditional values, and loyalty to duty. All of these things are important, but they do not save. Observing them does not reconcile persons to God. No matter how much we strive to obey every "thou shalt" that comes from the voice of God, we will never build up enough credits to merit salvation. Like Sysiphus pushing the rock up the hill, before he gets to the top, the rock slides back to the bottom. The Christian moralist sees Jesus as a second Moses, one who came to give a new law. What's wrong with this picture is that the entire relationship to God is constructed on juridical categories, in terms of law, rather than in terms of the grace and love of God.

The moralistic ladder must be torn down in order for a person to accept the grace of God in Christ through faith alone apart from the works of the law. The moralist is striving for righteousness. But Jesus said to the pharisees that their righteousness, good as it is, is not sufficient to make them right with God. The moralist stands erect before God and prays, "God, I thank you that I am not like those people over there." We should strive to be as good as the pharisees, knowing full well that that is not good enough. "For there is no distinction; since all have sinned, and fall short of the glory of God."[14]

Emotionalism in religion is a third ladder. A certain type of religious experience may be required for fellowship with God. Feeling the faith is what counts, and exhibiting emotions in worship is deemed to be most desirable. Worship is programmed to make people feel good. That is why some worship leaders take to using noisy sounds, rhythmic beats or psychological gimmicks, to make people feel like jumping up and down, waving their hands in the air, and dancing in the aisles. Televangelists know that it is easier to make a pitch for big bucks when listeners have been placed under a spell of mind-numbing feelings.

Feelings are important. We are all creatures of feeling. And if you feel like jumping up and down, go ahead and do it, but usually you will not feel comfortable doing it in a Lutheran church. As long as we are on a light note, there's a story about a man who attended a Lutheran church service. He got so excited about what the preacher was saying that he cried out, "Praise the Lord!" A person behind him leaned forward and whispered in his ear, "Sir, this is a Lutheran church. Here we don't praise the Lord."

The serious point is that as humans we are bound to have feelings, but as Lutherans we tend not to trust them very much. They can be so fickle and fleeting; they can pump you up one moment and then as quickly let you down. The gospel does not require any particular quality of experience or intensity of emotion to hear and heed the word of the Lord. The highly emotional temperament has no advantage over the stoic reserve of those who keep their feelings to themselves. My father was a good Norwegian. It was cold in Norway; you kept your hands in your mittens. I never saw him shed a tear, even though he had plenty of things to cry about.

It is solely on account of Christ who came down a ladder from heaven that we meet God at ground level. There we meet him at the foot of the cross, with not a leg to stand on. Christ alone is our ladder to heaven, so all the other ladders must come down. We do not need to climb any ladder to heaven, not even Jacob's ladder, whose every rung goes higher and higher. That is what the doctrine of justification by faith alone is all about. It is the one big thing, the one thing needful that Mary learned sitting at Jesus' feet.

Norms for a Christian Doctrine of Salvation

I will try to reduce the Christian doctrine of salvation to a few talking points, each of which can serve as an occasion for an extended conversation among theologians, as well as pastors and lay persons. I have a reason for doing this. It has been brought to my attention that official representatives have been defending the ELCA against the accusation of teaching universal salvation by quoting me.[15] Troubled lay people and pastors have written to inquire whether I have retracted my views on salvation. So here in a nutshell is what I teach and confess concerning the doctrine of salvation. Moreover, I believe it is in accord with the Lutheran confessions.

1. Only God can save. Human beings cannot save themselves, no matter how hard they try to be holy and acceptable to God. Every synergistic doctrine of salvation is a heresy. Everyone seems to be a natural-born Pelagian.

2. God's only saving bridge to the world is Jesus the Christ. He alone is the Mediator between God and the world. The gospel says there is no other name under heaven by which people can be saved.

3. An understanding of the death of Jesus on the cross (atonement) must take seriously the polarity between the justice and love of God. Love without justice is sentimentalism, and justice without love makes salvation of a guilty world impossible. Some doctrines of the atonement stress one without the other. Anselm wanted to satisfy justice; Abelard wanted to hear only of love. Other examples could be offered.

4. The whole life of Christ from his incarnation through his death, resurrection, and ascension to the right hand of God must be included in the story of our salvation. Lutherans have inherited the slogan *theologia crucis* and set it over against a *theologia gloria*. We would misconstrue the meaning of this distinction were we to make the mathematical point of the cross bear the whole burden of salvation. The cross without the resurrection of Jesus is not only not the whole gospel, it is no gospel at all.

5. The atonement is a once-for-all act that is inherently and antecedently valid, prior to any subjective response on the part of believers. Faith does not generate the efficacy of the salvation event; faith can only receive what is given by the grace of God.

6. The human predicament consists in sin as a guiltiness before the living God which can be rectified only by the act of forgiveness. Only salvation centered in Christ overcomes estrangement from God.

7. God's way of salvation is by means of his identification with sinful humanity. In classical atonement doctrine (e.g., Irenaeus and Athanasius), the incarnate Son of God became what we are so that we might become what he is. He came to participate in our humanity, so that we might participate in his divinity.

8. God's intention is to save the *whole* human race, not only a remnant thereof. "This is right and is acceptable in the sight of God our Savior, who desires *everyone* to be saved and to come to the knowledge of the truth" (I Tim. 2: 3-4). We are *all* descendants of Adam, wounded by original and hereditary sin. "For as in Adam all die, so also in Christ shall all be made

alive" (I Cor. 15:22). The question is: does all mean all, or does all mean only a few?

9. God in Christ bears the whole guilt of sin and all its consequences. The sinless Christ suffered the punishment of our sin; his is therefore a vicarious suffering.

10. By his suffering and death on the cross Christ won a victory over the tyrants that oppress the world. Salvation means liberation from the power of the Evil One and all his works and ways. Between Good Friday and Easter Sunday Christ was in hell "preaching to the spirits in prison" (I Pet. 3:19). What was he doing that for? Possibly to give them a "second chance." That is pure speculation. Nobody really knows. But many orthodox fathers have thought that it might be so. I believe that is about as far as a universalism of the gospel can stretch without ending up in some kind of gnosticism.

Chapter Two
Ecclesiology

T his chapter will deal with the doctrine of the church — ecclesiology. We will begin with a bit of etymology. Ecclesiology comes from two words, *ecclesia* and *logos*. *Ecclesia* is a Latin word that comes from two Greek words, *ek* meaning "out of" and *kaleo* meaning "to call." Thus, *ecclesia* is an assembly of persons whom God has called out of the nations, to make them his own people. Ecclesiology is the study of the church, its nature and attributes, how it is organized and what is its mission. So ecclesiology deals with the nature and purpose of the church.

The word "church," on the other hand, has a different etymological origin. Church is an English word that comes from the Greek word "*kuriake*," a word related to "*kyrios*," meaning "Lord." "*Kuriake*" is what belongs to the Lord. The German word is *Kirche*, the Swedish is *Kyrke*, and the Scottish is *Kerk*. The root meaning is that the church belongs to the Lord.

In English the word "church" is used in so many different ways, that no simple definition will cover its many meanings. Martin Luther said, "Thank God, any seven year old child knows what the church is." Really? Maybe in his day, but not today. For that child has heard his parents say, "We are going to church today." That suggests the church is an organized congregation, like Lake Wobegon Lutheran Church or Our Lady of Perpetual Responsibility in Lake Wobegon, Minnesota. The congregation belongs to a church with a particular denominational name, Lutheran or Catholic or some other.

Or, maybe we say, we have just built a new church, suggesting the church is a building made of bricks and mortar, or steel and glass. None of these is what the New Testament means by church.

The Beginnings of the Church

When we ask the question, "What is the church?" our search for an answer must start at the beginning. Before the birth of Jesus of Nazareth there was no church. There was Israel, the people of God in the Old Testament. The church makes its appearance in the New Testament as the new people of God, against the backdrop of Jesus' preaching of the kingdom of God. His life, death, and resurrection are portrayed in the Gospels as the in-breaking of God's kingdom proclaimed by Jesus. The church is not the kingdom of God; it is the community of hope poised between the times, the time of the initial breakthrough of the kingdom in Jesus and the time of his final advent at the end of history. This means that Jesus' message of the kingdom of God must be the point of departure for understanding what the church is. For this reason the church is often referred to as an eschatological event, sharing the eschatological orientation of the kingdom itself.

The kingdom horizon of the church means that the church does not exist from itself or for itself. The church exists *from* the kingdom of God which Jesus proclaimed and embodied in his own person and ministry; and it exists *for* the world for whose salvation Jesus died and was raised by God on the third day. Church-centeredness is always a great temptation. The church's concern for the world is not an after-thought. Rather, when the church prays daily for the coming of God's kingdom, she prays also that his will may be done on earth as it is in heaven. The church is the means by which the mission of the kingdom is carried out in and for the world. Because the church exists to serve the kingdom of God in history, it is pointed toward the world, as light to the nations and as the new humanity that Jesus inaugurated in his own person. The church exists as the chosen instrument of God's kingdom for the sake of the world and she loses her very reason for being if she abandons her missionary orientation to the world.

Article VII of the Lutheran *Augsburg Confession* defines the church as "the congregation of saints in which the Gospel is rightly taught and the Sacraments are rightly administered." This is a partial definition. What it says is important, even essential, but what it omits reveals a deficiency from which present-day Lutheranism still suffers. There is no mention in this classic definition of the church's orientation to the kingdom of God and of her missionary vocation in world history. A fuller definition of the church would include its being in polar tension between the kingdom of God and the world. The omission of explicit reference to the eschatological and missionary dimensions of the church's existence accounts for a serious blunder in the history of Lutheranism: the rejection of world missions in the period of seventeenth century scholasticism. To sum up: the starting point for a definition of the church must be Jesus' message of the kingdom of God and it must envision the world as the field of its mission. The mission to the nations is fundamental to the church's very being. We cannot define the nature of the church, then tack on its mission as optional activity. The being of the church is to exist as the function of the kingdom of God in the open field of world history.

The first generation of Christians encountered a huge problem of how to define the church. They debated the question whether the church is essentially an updated version of Israel, the people of God, or whether the church can accommodate Gentiles without holding them to the Jewish law of circumcision. When the apostle Paul opened the doors of the church to include Gentiles, that was the start of interminable conflict between Jewish and Gentile Christians that kept simmering beneath the surface until it exploded in the twentieth century holocaust. The holocaust happened partly because of the failure of Christianity to resolve the theological problem of the relationship between the two covenants of God with Israel and the Church. Supersessionism is the traditional belief held by some Christians that Jews are no longer the people of God. In this view the church is the new and true Israel, replacing the old Israel. Since Judaism does not believe Jesus is the Messiah, it was considered an ersatz religion, with no theological reason to be. This idea is largely to blame for the mistreatment of Jews.

The supersessionist ideology has a long history in the Christian tradition, based on a misinterpretation of Paul's letters by the second century heresiarch Marcion of Sinope (85-160 AD), a prominent early leader of Gnosticism. He was followed by other Gnostics such as Valentinus and Basileides, who wished to eliminate the Old Testament and everything Jewish from Christianity. To be sure, Paul did engage in a heated controversy with the leaders of his own people. The first Jewish Christians were centered mostly in Jerusalem and Palestine. They remembered Jesus and in some real sense believed in him; they also received the outpouring of the Holy Spirit at Pentecost. There were apostles among them. But Paul had serious questions about their teaching. He called them "false prophets" and "deceitful workers."[16] Once he referred to them as "super-apostles."[17] Worse yet, he called them "dogs,"[18] which in modern slang would be "sons of bitches."

Paul's argument with the Jewish Christians — also called "Judaizers" — was not only about circumcision and food taboos, but also about justification by faith apart from the works of the law. The book of James was most likely written by a Jewish Christian who aimed to counter Paul's emphasis on faith apart from works. Some commentators have tried to paper over the difference between Paul and James. They argue that since the Bible is the inspired and inerrant Word of God, everything in it must be harmonious, without any contradictions. Luther was not one of them. He called the book of James "an epistle full of straw" because it seemed to contradict Paul's teaching on justification by faith. Paul wrote, "For we hold that a person is justified by faith apart from the works of the law."[19] James wrote: "Show me your faith apart from your works, and I by my works will show you my faith.... You see that a person is justified by works and not by faith alone."[20] Is there any contradiction? For Paul, God justified Abraham on account of his faith apart from his works. For James, God justified Abraham not only because of his faith, but also his works. The point of bringing this up here is not to exonerate Luther, much less harmonize Paul and James, but only to show the radical difference between two kinds of Christianity emerging out of the first century, Jewish and Gentile Christianity.

Thousands of Jewish Christians still exist. They believe Jesus is the Messiah, obey the Torah, practice circumcision, observe the Sabbath, adhere to the dietary laws of Judaism, and wear the yarmulke. Jesus-believing Jews seem to be a thorn in the flesh of both Jews and Christians today, but I am very thankful for them. Their presence reminds us that Jesus was a Jew, the Messiah of Jewish expectation. The first Christians were all Jews. A church of Gentiles without Jews is an anomaly. It was never meant to happen, and their absence from Christian congregations is a tragic sign that the church is not as catholic as it confesses in its creed. The apostle Paul reminds the Gentiles that they are merely the wild shoot grafted onto the olive tree.[21]

How much blame can be placed on Paul for the anti-Judaism that has persisted in historic Christianity, both in the East and in the West? When Paul came down hard against the Judaizers — those who followed the basics of the law, circumcision and dietary rules — he did this for theological reasons. The Judaizers were attacking Paul as an illegitimate apostle. Who is Paul? Where did he get his authority? So Paul had to defend himself and his apostleship. He received his authority directly from the risen Christ whom he met on the road to Damascus. That opened the door for Paul to preach a gospel wrapped in Jewish garments to the Gentiles. Paul did not believe that it was necessary for Gentiles to become Jews first in order to become converts to Christ. Paul's gospel invited Gentiles to become adopted children of God through their faith in Jesus, without requiring them to keep the law binding on Jews.

The question was: Can an uncircumcised Gentile become a member of the people of God? Paul said, "Yes, of course!"

To be a Christian is to acknowledge that the law has been fulfilled in Jesus the Messiah. Hence, the Gentile believer is under no obligation to keep the law, such as the Sabbath, food taboos, and circumcision. The Judaizers said, "No way!" Faith in Jesus does not absolve a person from keeping the law. Jesus observed the law, including circumcision, and his followers should too. But here is the problem: If Gentiles are freed from the law, what is their motivation to behave in a moral and ethical way? Will not that lead to antinomianism, permitting Gentiles to disdain the law and to live any way that they choose? The result would be libertinism — living a life free from all moral restraints. But that is not what Paul meant. He composed a long list of sins, sins which are totally unacceptable to those who are in Christ Jesus, led by a new law, the law of love, manifest in the "fruits of the Spirit."

Regrettably, Paul's theological arguments have been wrongly used to fuel racial hostility and hatred of Jews. Germany is the land where Lutherans made the Pauline doctrine of justification by faith alone apart from the works of the law the article by which the church stands and falls. We Lutherans have based this on our reading of Paul's two important letters, Galatians and Romans. However, some Lutherans have shamelessly seen no contradiction between their acceptance of Paul's theology and their hatred of of the Jews. It seemed to them as if Paul's attack on the law justified their anti-Judaism.

A whole new can of worms has been opened up by a school of biblical scholars who are advancing a new perspective on Paul. In their opinion Luther's theology of justification by faith alone and its accompanying distinction between law and gospel were based on his mis-reading of Paul. The crux of the debate between the old perspective on Paul, stemming from Luther and Calvin, and the new perspective, conceived by E. P. Sanders, James Dunn, and N. T. Wright, has to do with what Paul meant by the "works of the law."

The new perspective asserts that by the "works of the law" Paul had in mind only the special badges of Jewish identity, the things that define what a Jew is, called "boundary markers," like circumcision, dietary rules, observation of the Sabbath, festival days and seasons. The old perspective argues that for Paul the "works of the law" are any human efforts to gain the favor of God, to merit salvation by the good works that a person does. It is called "works-righteousness," becoming righteous not by the imputation of God's righteousness on account of faith in the substitutionary sacrifice of Christ, but by doing enough good works to meet the demands of God's righteous expectations. Both perspectives are in favor of doing good works. For Luther faith alone never meant without good works. Luther and the old perspective maintains that God by grace endows individuals with the gift of faith which leads to a new life in Christ and good works. The new perspective holds that God by grace empowers individuals to faith and good works which then lead to salvation. In this view good works do count for something on the balance sheet of salvation. It is not surprising that Roman Catholic and Eastern Orthodox theologians favor the new perspective, because they have always included a dose of synergism or semi-Pelagianism in their understanding of salvation. Which side is right, the new or the old perspective on Paul? The debate is underway, and neither side can claim to have given the last word. Meanwhile, it may be readily conceded that Luther's criticism of the medieval system of meritorious works and Paul's argument against the "works of the law" are not to be equated. In any case, Luther's doctrine of justification by faith apart from the works of the law is not dependent on the outcome of the debate between the old and the new perspectives on Paul.

To turn our attention to another front, Gentile Christianity developed beyond Palestine and beyond Judaism. Gentile Christianity ceased to observe the Jewish Torah. Circumcision was no longer deemed necessary, but replaced by water baptism. Gentiles could eat what they wanted and eventually switched their church-going from Saturday to Sunday. The loss of its Hebrew roots made the gospel vulnerable to ideologies alien to the Scriptures. This happened in the early centuries when New Testament Christianity met the challenge of Gnosticism and the surrounding Hellenistic culture. Adolf von Harnack coined the phrase "the Hellenization of the Gospel" to criticize the development of dogma in the ancient church that led to the trinitarian and christological definitions of the Nicene and Chalcedonian Creeds. He failed to see that these very dogmas equipped the church with the needed arsenal to fight against the anti-Jewish polemics of the Gnostics. Von Harnack represented the anti-Judaism of German Protestant theology that approved of the racial policies of the Nazis. Harnack wrote: "The rejection of the Old Testament in the second century was an error which the great church rightly opposed; holding on to it in the sixteenth century was a destiny which the Reformation was not able to escape; but for Protestantism to preserve it since the nineteenth century as a canonical document is the result of a religious and ecclesiastical paralysis."[22]

At the same time that the early church was growing in the Hellenistic world, Judaism was developing side by side. It was the Judaism of the Pharisees. It is called Rabbinic Judaism, because it was led by the Rabbis. Other forms of Judaism that we read about in the New Testament withered and died out – the Zealots, the Essenes, and the Sadducees. The future belonged to the Pharisees. The two religious streams that emerged out of Palestine – Christianity and Judaism – began to define themselves in sharp opposition to each other. The poor Jewish Christians, known as Ebionites, got blackballed by both organized Christianity and Judaism and gradually withered away. The Ebionites held a low Christology. For them Jesus was a mere man, a prophet, yes, but not the Son of God. So they were no longer a challenge to orthodox catholic Christianity based on the preaching of the apostles and the primitive Christian mission to the Graeco-Roman world.

But a challenge did come from a completely opposite direction, from the world of Hellenistic mystery religions. The pagan religiosity in the Graeco-Roman world was syncretistic. Syncretism means to mix together beliefs and practices from many different religions, akin to the New Age mystical spirituality of today. Gnosticism is the name for this syncretistic religious phenomenon. When elements from the Bible and Christianity were added to the stew, the result is called "Gnostic Christianity." The best-seller novel by Dan Brown, *The Da Vinci Code*, gives a pretty good idea of what Gnostic Christianity was like. He filled his book with a lot of goofy beliefs from old-fashioned gnostic Christianity. One such was that Jesus was married to Mary Magdalene and fathered a son.

Gnostic Christianity is not dead. It is alive and well in America, especially in California and it thrives among the Hollywood intelligentsia. Gnosticism is a word that comes from "gnosis," which means "knowledge" in Greek. A gnostic is a person who believes that salvation is gained by accessing esoteric mysteries hidden from ordinary people. Gnostic Christianity held four basic beliefs. 1) The cosmos, the world, is made of two completely different things, spirit and matter. The upper spiritual reality was created by a good God; the lower material reality was created by a different God, an evil power, called the demiurge. 2) A human being is made of two parts, a heavenly soul indwelling a material body. The soul was a divine spark that got imprisoned within a blob of filthy flesh. 3) Salvation consists in liberating the immortal soul from the dungeon of this mortal body, to leave the world here below to the upper world of celestial paradise. 4) The only thing that Christianity added to this dualistic system was belief in Christ. Christ came down to earth to bring the saving knowledge or gnosis to the souls lost in material darkness.

When gnostic evangelists spread these beliefs, they made them sound so Christian and Christ-centered, that many gullible people swallowed them hook, line, and sinker. In 1945 an Egyptian peasant whose name was Mohammed Ali — not the famous boxer — ventured into some mountains in Egypt to look for natural fertilizer. He found a large earthenware jar which contained a number of leather bound documents. He brought them home and threw them on a pile of straw ready to use for kindling. Eventually they were rescued and taken to a museum, where scholars translated them from the Coptic language. Up until then we knew about Gnostic Christianity only from the polemical writings of orthodox fathers like Irenaeus, Tertullian, and Hippolytus, who described the gnostic beliefs they rejected as heresies. Recently scholars have had a heyday filling in the gaps of knowledge and have thereby constructed a rather complete picture of gnostic Christianity.

When John's gospel says that "the Word became flesh," that was an anti-gnostic assertion. The orthodox fathers said that the flesh is good. There is nothing the matter with matter, because God created it, and he did not create anything bad or evil. The orthodox fathers affirmed the goodness of the body. They believed in the resurrection of the body. Sanctification is not a process of becoming spiritual, in flight from our bodily existence.

The Four Pillars of the Emerging Catholic Church

By the third century orthodox catholic Christianity had pretty much silenced its opposition from both ends of the spectrum, from the side of Jewish Christianity and from the side of Gnostic Christianity, not without, however, absorbing elements of both in the process. There were basically four pillars on which the emerging catholic church was built.

The first pillar was the Creed. It was originally founded on the high Christology of John's Gospel, which led to the development of the doctrine of the Trinity. "In the beginning was the Word, and the Word was with God, and the Word was God.... And the Word became flesh."[23] Here we find the root of the confession that Jesus is God in the flesh, both fully divine and fully human. The earliest formal confession was the "rule of faith" (regula fidei), which forms the core of the Apostles' Creed.

The second pillar was the Canon, a selection of the apostolic writings, Gospels and Epistles, which formed the New Testament, by which all later traditions would be measured.

The third pillar is the cult, the Christian practice of worshipping God in the name of Jesus. This is the weekly remembrance of Jesus' death and resurrection, variously termed the Lord's Supper, Holy Communion, or the Eucharist. We should note that there never was a gathering for worship on the Sabbath that did not include the breaking of bread and sharing the cup to celebrate the presence of Jesus in the church. The theology of Holy Communion has changed from time to time, but the church's practice has invariably included eating bread and drinking wine at the Lord's Table in the belief that the living Christ is truly present.

The fourth pillar is Church Order, the institutional structuring that included a threefold ministry of bishops, presbyters, and deacons. Lutherans have often wasted a lot of breath discounting the importance of the Pastoral Epistles, I and II Timothy and Titus. These writings make clear that by the end of the first century the church had established a threefold ordering of its ministerial leadership. Those are the four pillars that formed the edifice of first century catholic Christianity.

The Apostles' Creed met a growing need for the church to distinguish the true faith from fake alternatives. Many who claimed to be followers of Jesus and the apostles were teaching doctrines which, when judged by the Creed, had to be rejected as heresies.

The office of bishop became increasingly important as the focus of the church's unity, with the responsibility to defend its faith from false teaching. The bishop was supposed to apply the "rule of faith" to distinguish between orthodoxy and heresy. Many ordinary Christians whose churches have leaders called "bishops" have asked: When did the bishops forget how to do what they are supposed to do — to care for the unity of the church and protect the truth of the faith? The notorious examples of Bishops Pike and Spong prove that there is no guarantee that bishops will be on the side of orthodoxy. This should remind us that many of the great heresies in the early church were named after bishops, for example, Arius, Sabellius, and Nestorius.

Within three centuries Catholic Christianity had emerged as the mainstream, marking it off from all competing and counterfeit forms. When Constantine, the head of the Roman Empire, made Christianity its official religion and condemned all others, such a victory came with a heavy price. New Testament Christianity was never aligned with the super-powers of the world. With Constantine Christianity was converted into Christendom, the state religion allied with worldly powers. That produced what political historians called "Caesaropapism" — a secular ruler holding supreme authority over both state and church. For the next millennium church history was to be dominated by the ensuing struggles for power between popes and emperors.

Images of the Church

The German bishop and theologian, Otto Dibelius, wrote a book entitled, *The Century of the Church*. He had in mind the twentieth century. It seems that church history is like a train going from one station to another. At each station the church pauses to deal with a major doctrinal conflict. In the first century the issue was the church's relation to the synagogue, especially whether Gentile believers must obey the Jewish law concerning circumcision and diet. In the second century the church had to face the threat of gnosticism. In the fourth century the church produced the trinitarian confession of the Nicene Creed. In the fifth century the church at Chalcedon confessed that Jesus Christ is one person in two natures, divine and human. The medieval church was involved in conflicts over sacramentology. The central focus of the Reformation was on soteriology, in particular, the doctrine of justification through faith alone, apart from the works of the law. It has fallen to the modern church to make the doctrine of the church — ecclesiology — its chief focus of attention.

Why has it taken the church twenty centuries to take up the question of its nature and purpose? The church has never promulgated an orthodox dogma on the church, distinguishing it from various possible heresies. The four marks of the church of the Nicene Creed — one, holy, catholic, and apostolic — were never set over against any heretical party in ancient Christianity. And no denomination in history or today has shown any inclination to reject any of the four marks for its own self-understanding. It is only when the churches in dialogue attempt to agree on precise dogmatic statements that controversial issues come to the fore.

Up until the Second Vatican Council it was widely assumed that the Roman Catholic Church possessed a fully developed concept of the church. But the proceedings and deliberations at the Council showed that this was not the case. New insights emerged at the Council due to vastly improved methods of biblical inquiry as well as to the feeling that a rigidly hierarchical and monarchical view of the church was ill-equipped to face the challenges of the modern world. The summons to new thinking was encapsulated in two words, *resourcement* (return to the ancient sources) and *aggiornamento* (bringing the church up-to-date). The French have a saying: *il faut reculer pour mieux avancer* ("It's necessary to go backward to better go forward"). That is what the bishops and theologians did at Vatican II to make its outcome so profound and enduring.

Paul Minear, who taught New Testament at Yale Divinity School, wrote a book that is now a classic, *Images of the Church in the New Testament.*[24] The word "images" conveys the fact that the New Testament does not give us definitions or doctrines of the church in propositional terms, with a subject and a predicate. What we find are word-pictures, metaphors, and images that reflect the Hebraic way of thinking rather than the Greek. The Hebrews gave us history with its concrete stories about events and persons. The Greeks gave us philosophy with its abstract speculations about ideas and essences. Reading the Old Testament — Genesis, Exodus, or Deuteronomy — is very different from reading the Greek philosophers — Plato or Aristotle. We have no definitions of the church in the New Testament. Instead, we have a host of images. We have a gallery of pictures that can open our minds to see things some-

61

times better than by using propositional language. Paul Minear found 96 images of the church in the New Testament. Most of them are minor, with only a few biblical references, but that does not mean they are unimportant. Three of them convey the total dependence of the church on her Lord Jesus Christ. One is the image of the vine and the branches. The vine is the life-support of the branches. Jesus is the vine; his followers are the branches. A second is of the sheep and the shepherd. The sheep know the voice of the shepherd and follow him. A true shepherd lays down his life for the sheep. (That's the saying, but aren't shepherds more important than sheep?) A third is of the church as the house of God, with Christ as the corner-stone of the building. If the cornerstone is not true, the build-ing will not have straight walls or square corners.

Equally familiar are the images of the church as the people of God, the body of Christ, the temple of the Spirit, the bride of Christ, the family of God, the community of saints, the new creation, and so forth. Most of these images were drawn from the Old Testament to speak of the new community that came into being after Easter. The Synoptic Gospels — Matthew, Mark, and Luke — tell the story of Jesus and his message of the kingdom of God. They contain more than one hundred references to the kingdom of God. Dr. Luke wrote two books of the New Testament, the Gospel named after him and the Acts of the Apostles — the first chapter of church history.

The kingdom of God was the central theme of Luke's Gospel. Everything that Jesus said and did was related to the kingdom of God. But when Luke wrote the book of Acts, he scarcely made any mention of the kingdom. Why is there such a big difference between the the Gospel of Luke and the Book of Acts, both written by the same author? Why the remark-able change in subject matter? There can be only one correct answer. The difference was due to Easter, the resurrection of Jesus from death to new life. When Jesus preached the king-dom of God, he did not preach himself. After Easter, when the apostles preached, they did not preach the kingdom of God; they preached Jesus Christ, the crucified and risen Lord.

Because of Easter, Jesus' message of the kingdom of God was dramatically transformed into the message about Christ the King. Jesus the preacher of God's coming kingdom became the personal subject matter of the apostles' preaching.

Alfred Loisy, the French Catholic modernist, wrote: "Jesus foretold the kingdom, and it was the church that came."[25] How did the kingdom that Jesus preached become the church that he founded? How did Jesus' talk about the kingdom become the apostles' talk about the church in a matter of only a decade? Isn't the church we know from its history a far cry from the vision of the kingdom we see in Jesus' parables and sayings? The best explanation I know is the following: When Jesus preached the coming kingdom of God, the *basileia*, the Jews of his time understood what he was saying. Jews expected that when the Messiah comes, he would establish the reign of God. In the mind of the Jews, the Messiah and the kingdom go together like hand in glove. They could not think of one without the other. Orthodox Jews still speak of the Messiah and the kingdom in the same breath. What did Jesus have in mind when he talked about the kingdom? As a good Jew Jesus expected that God would overthrow the dominion of Satan and create a new world of lasting righteousness and blessedness. Jesus expected that God would establish the power and glory of his kingdom on earth, as it is in heaven. The prayer he taught his disciples says as much: "Thy kingdom come, thy will be done, on earth as it is in heaven." What did Jesus mean, what did the disciples think he meant, and what do we mean when we pray that prayer today?

What does all this talk about the kingdom have to do with the church? It is crucial to understand the connection. When the kingdom comes, everything is supposed to change. Things cannot remain the same. God's coming rule is the power to destroy all resistance to his will. And his will is to grant his gracious love to people in desperate need of a new beginning — poor people, tax collectors, and prostitutes. Poor people will have plenty, when the kingdom comes. The hungry will be satisfied and those who weep will jump for joy. There will be a turnabout of all things, when the kingdom comes. God's kingdom will come about as a result of his doing, not by people becoming more religious and doing the best they can. Nor will it come by military might or political conquest. That is what the messianic Jews expected in praying for the coming of God's kingdom. When that happens the Romans would be kicked out of the Holy Land, and the Jews would be free. Jesus was a messianic Jew in believing that God was coming soon in power and glory to put an end to suffering, misery, poverty, oppression, hunger, and even death.

But we know what actually happened. The hopes of Jesus and his disciples were shattered on the cross. The friends and followers of Jesus went away from Jerusalem, downcast and saddened by the events of Good Friday. They said, "We had hoped that Jesus would redeem Israel."[26] They had hoped that God would bring in the kingdom to put things right. But things did not come to pass as expected. Jesus died and the hope for the coming of God's kingdom was buried along with him. If that would have been the end of the story, the church would not have come into existence. There would have been no Christian faith. But that was not the end of the story. With the resurrection of Jesus and the outpouring of the Spirit on the day of Pentecost, something remarkable occurred. A few of Jesus' friends interpreted his death and resurrection as the initial breakthrough of the kingdom, as a down payment of the kingdom whose coming Jesus announced. Why? Because, when the kingdom comes, even the dead are made alive. Paul wrote, "But in fact Christ has been raised from the dead, the first fruits of those who have fallen asleep."[27] Just so, the risen Jesus is the down payment — the first fruits — of the in-breaking of the kingdom that founded the church.

The truth is — without Easter there would be no church! Without the resurrection, Jesus would have been just another forgotten messianic pretender whose hopes and prayers for the kingdom went unfulfilled. One timely reason to stress that Easter is the necessary precondition for the beginning of the church is that some modern Protestant theologians are trying to account for the rise of Christian faith without belief in the resurrection of Jesus. Adolf von Harnack, the great German church historian, wrote a popular and very influential book on the essence of Christianity, *Das Wesen des Christentums*, that sold in the millions. Its central thesis was that all the talk about the cross and resurrection of Jesus was an invention of the apostle Paul. The real essence of Christianity is supposedly based on the religion and ethics of Jesus, which Harnack summed up as the Fatherhood of God and the infinite value of the human soul.[28]

Harnack's thesis has been renewed by some of the scholars of the so-called "Jesus Seminar."[29] Their proposal is to base a new Christianity on what Jesus stood for before he died on the cross. Robert Funk, the founder of the "Jesus Seminar," called for a return to Jesus minus reference to his cross and resurrection. He writes that we have "to start all over again with a clean theological slate, with only the parables, aphorisms, parabolic acts, and deeds of Jesus as the basis on which to formulate a new version of the faith."[30]

We have dealt with the image of the kingdom of God as the starting point for understanding how the church came into being and what it is. But there are other important images. A popular one in Roman Catholic and Anglican theology is the "body of Christ," indicating that just as "no man is an island," so also there is no such thing as an isolated Christian who exists on his own sheltered island. From the start each person is baptized into the body of Christ and becomes one of many co-equal members. Baptism was not a Christian innovation. Jews were doing baptisms before Christians. Jesus himself was baptized by a Jew, John the Baptizer. The earliest Christian baptism was done in the name of Jesus. Later the formula was expanded to include the Triune name of God, Father, Son, and Holy Spirit. But baptism by itself is of no value apart from repentance and faith. Some missionaries were accused of taking a fire hose to a village and baptizing everyone in one fell swoop. That is, of course, a caricature of the belief in the regenerative efficacy of baptism. As Luther taught in his *Small*

Catechism that without the Word of God the water is merely water and no baptism. But when connected with the Word of God it is a baptism. Properly understood, baptism and faith belong together, whether faith comes before baptism, as in the case of adults, or after the act, as in the case of infants. "He who believes and is baptized will be saved; but he who does not believe will be condemned."[31]

Paul uses the image of the body to admonish members of the community to live in unity, harmony, and mutual support. Though the body is one, it has many members. All are important. The eye cannot say to the hand, I have no need of you, nor can the hand say to the feet, I have no need of you. If one member suffers, all suffer together. In a lengthy passage in I Corinthians Paul drives home the point that the whole church is the body of Christ made up of individual members who are indispensable to each other.

Every body has a head. Christ is the head of the body. The total Christ is the body and head together, stressing their indivisible relationship. Where Christ is, there is the church, and where the church is, there is Christ. One does not exist without the other. The body is one. What happens when some of the members mess up? Paul warned that false teachers would come and endanger the unity of the body of Christ. Unity is threatened by the preaching of a different gospel. In short, unity is fractured by heresy.

Heresy is a notoriously difficult topic, because every Christian teacher is a heretic in somebody else's eyes. Paul was condemned as a heretic by the Judaizers. The first Jews who believed in Jesus were considered heretical by the rulers of the Jerusalem synagogue. Christianity was at first regarded as a Nazarene sect and a Jewish heresy. The word "heresy" means to choose for oneself, to opt for an individual opinion that deviates sharply from the consensus of the established community. By an act of excommunication heretics were traditionally excluded from church fellowship. Nowadays heretics often are authors of best-sellers and popularly celebrated as heroes for defying authority and thinking novel thoughts.

But something terrible happened in the history of heresy. From the time of Constantine, orthodox Christianity became an imperial church, a state religion. In time that brought with it what is called the "inquisition" against heretics. Any violation of orthodoxy was met by cruel opposition. When Christians were in the minority in the pagan Roman Empire, they pleaded for tolerance. When they became the powerful majority, they forgot about tolerance. The persecuted church became the persecuting church. The inquisition was a medieval institution of the Roman Catholic Church charged with the eradication of heresies. It represents the darkest chapter in all of church history. It is important for the church to remember not only its glory days but also its darkest times. The inquisition was the worst of those times. When we confess that the church of Christ is holy, we must also confess that it is a church of sinners. Nothing bears that out more gruesomely than the grisly flames the inquisition kindled at the stake.

When we visited Dachau and Buchenwald, we could not believe our eyes and ears. What we have read about the actions of bishops and popes of the Middle Ages, with the secular support of kings and emperors, is equally unbelievable. Heretics were tortured until their confessions were forced out of them. Visiting museums in Europe we saw the instruments of torture used against thousands of heretics. The practice of the inquisition to root out all heresy was not abolished in the Catholic states of southern Europe until the nineteenth century. We have to wonder, how could it be that the church of the Prince of Peace could become collectively so psychopathic and neurotic that it would use force as a means of church discipline, that it would condone spreading and preserving the true faith by fire and sword, that it would use the Bible to justify the torture and murder of dissenters who did not believe in the orthodoxy of the time?

Heresy is a problem for the church. Like a virus it is bad for the health of the body. If we are honest with ourselves, we will confess that there is a bit of the heretic in each one of us, as well as a bit of the inquisitor. Heresy has been with the church from the beginning. Bishops and theologians have never figured out a salutary way to deal with it. A minority of voices has always counseled against the use of force, like Chrysostom, Ambrose, Francis of Assisi, and Benedict. Since the Enlightenment religious tolerance has become the only acceptable policy. No church today treats heretics with physical violence, even though heresies flourish in the church more than ever. The problem for the church is that, on the one hand, heresies are not acceptable and, on the other hand, churches do not know how best to oppose them. In Chicago Cardinal Bernadin was asked why he does not discipline the Catholic heretics in his diocese. He answered that if he does, that will make them even more popular. The Roman Catholic Church is the one church that attempts at the highest level to exclude heresies, but with mixed results. The Vatican silences the heretics, renders them incommunicado, and denies them permission to teach theology in a Catholic school. Some of them comply, while others get a good job in a Protestant seminary.

Israel's favorite self-designation was the "people of God." God said to Moses, "I am the Lord. I will deliver you from your bondage in Egypt. I will take you for my people, and I will be your God."[32] This refrain runs throughout the history of Israel. I am the Lord your God. I have chosen you to be my people. I have made a covenant with you. You are a people set apart. God makes tiny Israel the focal point of world history. God promised Israel a land and gave it to them. But the history of Israel, according to its own prophets, is a story of failures, betrayals, and loss of faith. It is also a story of the sin of idolatry. Thus the way was prepared for the story of redemption and renewal by the coming of God's kingdom in Jesus' life, ministry, death, and resurrection. The first Christians claimed the image for themselves; they are the new people of God. The original people of God — the Jews — still exist and the two peoples will co-exist until the end of history, when as Paul writes, "All Israel will be saved."[33]

The difference between the New Testament people of God — Christians — and the Old Testament people of God — Jews

— is that the new people of God come from all the nations, from all the races, classes, cultures, and religions. A person can be born a Jew, African, white, or wealthy, but a person cannot be born a member of the new people of God. To become a Christian a person must be "born again." So the church can never be a caste or class of like-minded ethnocentric religious people. God gathers his church from around the world, from every nation, language, class, race, and religion. Christianity is the only truly universal and international religion known in world history. Islam is the only other religion that could plausibly make the same claim.

The temple of the Holy Spirit is another image of the church. The Holy Spirit makes a person a member of the body of Christ. No one has said it better than Martin Luther in his explanation of the Third Article of the *Apostles' Creed*:

> I believe that by my own reason or strength I cannot believe in Jesus Christ, my Lord, or come to him. But the Holy Spirit has called me through the Gospel, enlightened me with his gifts, and sanctified and preserved me in true faith, just as he calls, gathers, enlightens, and sanctifies the whole Christian Church on earth and preserves it in union with Jesus Christ in the one true faith. In this Christian Church he daily and abundantly forgives all my sins, and the sins of all believers, and on the last day he will raise me and all the dead and will grant eternal life to me and to all who believe in Christ. This is most certainly true.

The apostle Paul wrote to the Christian community in Corinth: "Do you not know that you are God's temple and that God's Spirit dwells in you?"[34] In pagan religion God was thought to be dwelling in temples made of stone. Paul says that God lives in the church, the people of God, the body of Christ. Members of the community of Christ are the living stones of the temple of the Holy Spirit. But even such an ennobling idea can be corrupted. Since we have received the Spirit, perhaps we can devise means to control what the Spirit does, to do our bidding on our terms. The Spirit bestows gifts on individuals, to heal, perform miracles, speak in tongues, and drive out demons (exorcism). Some people in the church claim to possess such ecstatic and sensational endowments, while others do not. These same sorts of exceptional phenomena are reported to have been experienced by people in the ancient mystery religions. Paul was not opposed to these charismatic gifts as such. He confessed that he also had the gift of speaking in tongues and the apostles possessed the gift of healing. Paul wrote: "I thank God that I speak in tongues more than you all; nevertheless, in church I would rather speak five words with my mind, in order to instruct others, than ten thousand words in a tongue."[35]

I once heard a Pentecostal preacher use the analogy of a three story house. Some people live on the first floor. They are the adherents of the religions who believe in God the Creator of all things. Such are First Article of the Creed believers — Jews, Muslims, Deists, Unitarians, etc. Some live on the second story. They are the mass of ordinary Christians who believe in Jesus Christ and belong to the mainstream denominations — Catholics, Anglicans, Lutherans, and Protestants in general. They are Second Article of the Creed Christians. Then there are those who live on the third story, Christians of the Third Article of the Creed. They are the super-Christians who have been blessed by the Holy Spirit and have received the outpouring of the Pentecostal gifts.

Paul's letters to the Christians at Corinth tell about the pile of troubles he encountered by some of the congregational leaders who thought they were superior to the regular *hoi polloi* members. Paul said that there are many different spirits; there are even evil spirits. The discernment of spirits is itself a gift of the Holy Spirit.[36] Paul taught that there are two criteria for recognizing the work of the Spirit that comes from God. The first criterion is the ability to confess Jesus as Lord. The second criterion is the ability to serve the community, to edify it and build it up for the common good, such as acts of mercy, teaching, and helping others.

Spiritualistic movements have erupted in the church ever since the first century, such as the Montanists in the second century and the Joachimites in the Middle Ages, named after Joachim of Flora. He was a Cistercian abbot in the twelfth century who developed an interesting trinitarian interpretation of history that Jürgen Moltmann has re-worked into his own messianic eschatology.[37] Joachim divided history into three parts, modeled on the Trinity. The Old Testament represented the age of the Father. The history of the Catholic Church dominated by priests represented the age of the Son. The age of the Spirit dawned with monasticism, dominated by monks. In the age of the Spirit there will be no need for priests and bishops. People will be endowed with the wisdom of the Spirit. The Sermon on the Mount will be the rule of life. There will be no more war, and the spirit of peace, poverty, and humility — the monastic virtues — will triumph. The Jews will be converted and the Eastern and Western Churches will be reunited. Joachim never explained where the next generation of believers would come from, if everyone became a monk or a nun.

At the time of the Reformation Martin Luther, like the apostle Paul, had to deal with a lot of trouble coming from the people he called "enthusiasts." The German word is *Schwärmer*. While Luther was defending himself against Rome, he got hit from the other side, from the enthusiasts led by Thomas Müntzer (1488-1525). Müntzer was one of Luther's earliest followers, but he radicalized Luther's ideas. He believed that he was directly enlightened by the Holy Spirit and thus had an inside track in understanding the Bible. He believed he could turn the dead letters of the Bible into living words. Luther became very disgusted with the enthusiasts, many of them his former friends. Having in mind that the dove is the biblical symbol for the Spirit, Luther opined, "They have swallowed the Holy Spirit, feathers and all." Thomas Müntzer led a rebellion of the peasants against the princes, was captured, tortured, and executed.

Luther could not accept the main idea of the spiritual enthusiasts. They placed their private revelations from the Holy

Spirit above the once-for-all revelation of God in Jesus Christ according to the Scriptures, for all to read and understand. For them the Third Article of the Creed about the Holy Spirit trumped the Second Article about Jesus Christ. The enthusiasts loved in particular the *Book of Revelation* from which they derived many of their most fanciful ideas. They frightened and fascinated gullible and pious folks with their speculations about the approaching apocalyptic catastrophe. They had a lot to say about the world soon coming to an end in a ball of fire, about Armageddon and the Rapture. For Luther the work of the Holy Spirit is to lead us to the gospel of Christ, not to lure us into wild speculations about the end-time. There is no biblical promise that the Holy Spirit will deliver new revelations, new doctrines, new prophecies, which surpass the revelation of God in Jesus Christ. According to the Gospel of John, Jesus said that the Spirit "will bring to remembrance" everything that he has said.[38] The Spirit will not "speak on his own authority."[39] He will "glorify Christ."[40] He will take all that the Father has given to his Son and declare it to his followers.[41]

Thomas Müntzer and his followers represented what historians call the "Radical Reformation" or the "Left Wing Reformation." They are also known as Anabaptists. For the most part they do not play an active role in the ecumenical movement. They reject infant baptism, because they regard it as an institution of the state church. In Christendom everyone got baptized; it went along with citizenship. Anabaptism means re-baptism. Those baptized as infants must be re-baptized to become members of an Anabaptist community. In Anabaptist theology the relationship between the Word and the Spirit is rather loose, as compared to the mainstream of the Christian tradition. They trust in their private interpretations of the Bible, rather than being guided by the classical creeds and confessions of the church. Meanwhile the Spirit-movements — Pentecostal and Independent churches — are growing rapidly around the world, especially in the Global South. What impact this will have on the future of world Christianity is a subject of intense interest.[42]

Marks of the Church

In the Nicene Creed we confess that "we believe in the one, holy, catholic, and apostolic church." These four attributes are intended to help us to distinguish a true from a false church. When you move to a new city and shop around for a church to join, you want to know whether the church you are visiting is an authentic Church of Christ, or some offbeat sect. So what do you do? You look for signs, for certain distinguishing marks. And you ask, "Does this congregation have the marks of the true church, one, holy, catholic, and apostolic?" If you can say "yes," all other things being equal, you can in good conscience choose to become a member of that church and trust your family to its teaching. If you must say "no," then you won't want to join, no matter how attractive the church may appear in other respects.

But you have a problem. In the contemporary situation of denominational pluralism, there are so many churches not in fellowship with each other, all of them claiming with equal conviction that they are part of the one, holy, catholic, and apostolic church. They lay claim to the same marks, the identical attributes. Martin Luther and the other Reformers stressed their adherence to the creeds of the ancient church, the Apostles' Creed, the Nicene Creed, and the Athanasian Creed, word for word the same as they share with their Roman Catholic critics. Luther and the other Reformers argued, in effect, that just because you claim that yours is a true church with the traditional marks does not necessarily make it so. That is when Luther and Melanchthon added an additional criterion of the true church: "where the Gospel is purely taught and the Sacraments are rightly administered." Here the word "purely" means according to the Scriptures, and the word "rightly" means according to our Lord's institution. The Reformed and Anglican Churches followed the Lutheran Church in this respect.

Luther and the other Reformers were convinced that the gospel was obscured in the preaching and teaching of the late medieval Catholic Church, the church in which they were baptized, confirmed, and ordained. The practice of indulgences was a case in point. Roman Catholic theologians today admit that the church really did need to be reformed. Many abuses had to be corrected. But this Lutheran criterion, "where the gospel is purely preached and the sacraments are rightly administered" did not solve the problem either, because the radical reformers on the left, the enthusiasts, made exactly the same claim. They also claimed that they were restoring the pure preaching of the gospel according to the Scriptures and were administering the sacraments the way Jesus instituted them.

The rest is history. For the next four to five hundred years, all the churches quarreled and wrangled over the question of the true church. Every church has claimed for itself the classical adjectives — one, holy, catholic, and apostolic. Protestants stopped using the word "catholic," and instead used its synonym "universal." Even some Lutherans got upset when new hymn books restored the word "catholic" to the Creeds, to return to the original. Why surrender the word "catholic" to those who are loyal to Rome? Lutherans are not Roman Catholics, to be sure, but they are Catholics — Evangelical Catholics of the *Augsburg Confession*. The word "catholic" is in the ancient creed; the word "Roman" is not. The claim of the *Augsburg Confession* is that we are not inventing a new church named after a human being. We are not adding anything new that contradicts the Scriptures or the creeds of the ancient church.

Whether one thinks of the church as a body or as a people, it cannot survive without nourishment. The church lives from the Word of God presented to the Christian community by means of sacraments. The basic axiom of sacramentology is that "a sacrament does what it says and says what it does."[43] A sacramental sign or symbol participates in the reality to which it points. A sermon — composed of audible words — is sacramental because it conveys the real presence of the Word of God in the power of his Spirit. Preaching the gospel is spreading the good news of the kingdom of God already present in Jesus, the incarnate Word of God. The Word is a two-edged sword — law and gospel. Sin is the target of preaching the law,

74

because sin obstructs the way God intends human beings to live. The Word of God as law brings judgment against everything opposing the will and commandments of God. Such a word is searing and painful. Luther experienced that in such a moment it may be hard to tell whether one is being assaulted by God or the Devil. The word of the gospel is the exact opposite; it opens the hand of God's grace, love, and forgiveness, creating a pathway to new things, hope for a new world, a new humanity, and a new creation. Faith is a gift of the Spirit that enables us to know and accept the absolving word of the gospel as the absolute truth — no ifs, ands, or buts about it.

Holy Communion is a sacrament of the kingdom of God; it is also called the Lord's Supper — a miniature meal at which eating and drinking are taking place, in anticipation of the messianic banquet in the end-time. The banquet of the Messiah is for all the nations. The Lord invites into his fellowship (*koinonia*) the many who are sick and sinful to make them whole and holy. When we celebrate Holy Communion, we remember the death of Jesus on the cross. However, this meal is something more than a memorial of the Last Supper. That might be a fitting observance if ours were a dead Messiah. Then gloom and not joy would be called for. When we Christians gather to eat and to drink, we are not playing at being disciples in the Upper Room. We are not merely reenacting the historical drama of the last meal with Jesus. Instead, our remembrance of Jesus engenders joy because he was raised to be present with us as the living Lord of the universe. We experience new life in Christ and we embrace God's promise of the coming new age.

Holy Baptism is a sacramental act of putting off the old and taking on the new. It is founded on the death and resurrection of Jesus the Messiah. Baptism involves the individual in the drama of the shifting of the aeons. This is well symbolized when baptism is done by immersion. When individuals go under the water, that signals an end to the rule of sin, death, and the devil. When they come up, they turn away from the old and face the future under the lordship of Jesus. Baptism

75

empowers a person to struggle against the old order of existence in exchange for walking in a new direction pleasing to God.

Prayer is the language of hope for the coming of God's kingdom. The Psalms are filled with prayers that call upon God to keep the promises he made to his people Israel. In prayer we wrestle with God in the agony of the contradiction between the negativities of our experience here and now and what we expect when God will make all things new. We together with the world around us are not yet what we ought to be, not yet what we shall become when God will have brought all things to the fulfillment he has predestined for us and the world. Prayer is the groaning of the soul: "How long, O Lord, how long?" The "Amen" of prayer is the assurance of faith that God will be true to his word. Because God delivered his word to the world in the name of Jesus, we name his holy name in summoning God to remember us according to the generosity of his grace and mercy.

Whereas Lutherans traditionally think of the church in terms of Word and Sacraments, they also share the confession of the *Nicene Creed* that the church is one, holy, catholic, and apostolic. What church is the Creed talking about? There is no one church; there are many that claim to be the true church. There is no one holy church; every church is filled with sinners and hypocrites, and some with holy rollers. There is no one catholic church; many particular churches exist, each with its own distinctive history that often keeps it separated from others. And every church would like to think of itself as apostolic, yet there are so many dead churches scarcely engaged in the mission of the apostles to all the nations.

So what sense does it make to confess our belief in the one, holy, catholic, and apostolic church? These assertions about the church are paradoxical because their truth is contrary to what our ordinary eyes can observe. We introduce our confession with the words, "We believe." We see the truth of these assertions with the eyes of faith, not by sight. Before we confess our faith in the church as one, holy, catholic, and apostolic, we have already confessed our faith in Jesus Christ, the only begotten Son of God, true God and true man.

The Church is One. It is on account of Christ that we say the church is one, because the church is his body. Christ has only one body, with many members who are as different from each other as an arm and a leg. Whoever believes in Jesus as Lord and Savior and is baptized in the name of the Holy Trinity — Father, Son, and Holy Spirit — becomes a member of the body of Christ, no matter what the denominational label of the church one attends.

The church is in the Creed because it is part of the gospel. The whole gospel is about Christ, but not without his church. Christ is the head of the church and the church is the body of Christ. The head and the body belong together. There is nothing we can do to make the church one. The church is already one in Christ. All we can do with our ecumenical dialogues and concordats is to discover better ways to express our ecclesial unity in Christ. So why is this unity such a big deal? There is only one answer that matters, given in the words of Jesus — "that they may all be one ... so that the world may believe."[44] Church unity is for the sake of world mission. It is not merely bad manners but theologically inappropriate for any denomination to boast of being the one and only true church of Jesus Christ. That would be like one member of the body claiming to be the whole, with no need of any others.

Here is a heavy phrase one hears from time to time — ecclesiological docetism. Docetism is the ancient heresy, commonly attributed to the Gnostics, that Jesus only seemed to have a physical body, that in reality he was merely a spiritual and invisible essence. Applied to the church, it would be docetic to claim that the true church is invisible (*ecclesia invisibilis*), and that therefore church structures are matters of indifference. That would be a misinterpretation of the concept of the "invisible church." The true church is said to be invisible in contrast to the visible church which contains a mixture of the saved and the lost, a distinction known only to God. This distinction between the invisible and visible church does not mean that the church can exist in history without structures that give expression to the faith, hope, and love that drive Christians to be obedient in their mission to the world. Since Christianity is an historical social reality, it will always embody itself in concrete visible structures. To talk about the unity of the church, therefore, in strictly spiritualistic terms is the heresy of ecclesiological docetism.

So why not stick with the traditional structures of the church that have been tried and tested in the course of two millennia of history? Are all church structures created equal? Should heirs of the Reformation be more ready to adopt novel structures invented by modern sects and denominations than to retain those that are continuous with the great tradition of classical Christianity, East and West? Should the church re-invent itself in every generation? Is every office of the church and its ministry up for grabs? Should the church be open to the future in a way that cuts its links to the past? The answer to these questions is where the ecumenical rubber hits the road.

In my view Christian churches should seek to overcome their divisions by equipping themselves with structures recognizably continuous with the traditional offices of ministry, including episcopal and papal, provided these are reformed to serve the gospel and sacrifice all self-serving authoritarian features. The Encyclical of John Paul II, *Ut Unum Sint*, definitely points in this direction, but the aims of this document are far from being enacted. Meanwhile, Lutherans today should make clear that they have no doctrinal objections to the papal and episcopal offices as such, but only to the false doctrinal claims and the exercise of authoritarian power which developed in the Middle Ages. That is what the Reformers of the sixteenth century aimed to do. These structures will never be replaced by others, but they can be transformed to serve as representative signs of the continuity of the church with Jesus and the apostles and as special agencies to care for the self-identity of the church through the discontinuities of the historical process. Their task is to oversee the transmission of traditions faithful to the Scriptures to every new generation. No church can survive without leaders. But for the sake of the gospel there must be leadership without authoritarianism, disciplined life without coerced obedience, unity without uniformity, and freedom of inquiry without blind fideism.

The *Constitution on the Church* of Vatican II did not succeed in emancipating itself from its traditional authoritarian way of speaking "On the Hierarchy." The ancient Roman juridical mindset was still in control of this chapter. Vatican II missed the opportunity to formulate a doctrine that followed through on the initiative of Pope John XXIII to be the servant of servants. Moreover, *Ut Unum Sint* suggests that it is time for Roman Catholics to listen to the voice of Protestants who call for rethinking the dogma of papal infallibility. In this important encyclical Pope John Paul II echoed the words of his predecessor Pope Paul VI, who said in 1967: "We are aware that the pope is undoubtedly the greatest obstacle in the path of the Oecumene." Roman Catholics are invited to struggle with the dogma of papal infallibility and the exercise of papal authority in a way not unlike the struggle of Protestants with the doctrine of a verbally inerrant Bible and its infallible authority. Both sides may become convinced that infallible authorities, inerrant writings, and absolute ideologies are inadequate substitutes for the faithfulness of God to keep the promises he has given his people to accept on trust with the courage of hope. To speak of the infallibility of the church is not wrong, but we must be aware that it is a roundabout way of referring to the unfailing action of God's grace in keeping Jesus' promise that "the gates of Hades will not prevail against the church."[45] "Indefectibility" has been suggested as an acceptable term to express this promise of our Lord. By analogy a similar case can be made for the infallibility of the Bible. Our Lutheran confessions maintain that the Holy Scriptures are perfectly clear and trustworthy with respect to their purpose.

The Church is holy. In our day and age it is paradoxical to confess that the church is holy. There is no church without sin. Every church is filled with sinners and hypocrites. The holiness of the church is not a moral attribute that she possesses for all eyes to see. Holiness is a quality received by the church through its participation in the righteousness of Christ. As members of Christ's body we are called to be holy, and we believe the Holy Spirit is working to sanctify every member of the church. Every day we pray in the *Lord's Prayer* for the forgiveness of sins. And the next day we start over and struggle to bring forth the fruits of faith pleasing to God.

Luther's idea of the Christian as simultaneously "saint and sinner" (*simul iustus et peccator*) applies also to the church, every church. The apostle Paul addressed the Christians in Corinth as "saints," and then proceeded to berate them on account of their sins. He did the same to the Christians in Ephesus, Philippi, and Colossae. He called them "saints," and yet he assailed them for all their pettiness, legalism, quarrelsomeness, and imperfections. The *Westminster Confession* of the Reformed tradition states it well: "The purest churches under heaven are subject to mixture and error." There can be no doubt about it. All we need to do is read the newspaper headlines that publicize the heresies of Anglican bishops, the marital infidelities of Evangelical televangelists, the sexual misconduct of Catholic priests, and Lutheran pastors engaging in homosexual behavior, and with their church's stamp of approval to boot. Even the so-called Holiness Churches are not spared the embarrassing disclosures of immoral behavior on the part of some of their popular leaders.

In Roman Catholicism some specially spiritual and exemplary Christians are declared to be saints. The Vatican is busy these days trying to bestow sainthood on Mother Teresa. The process was well underway until conservative critics began to question her orthodoxy and her posthumous diaries disclosed her nagging doubts about God and the hope of salvation. Like mystics before her, she experienced a crisis of faith, the dark night of the soul (St. John of the Cross).

Reports also circulate that John Paul II is on a fast track to be declared a saint. The process by which a person becomes a saint in the Roman Catholic tradition is called "canonization." There are three stages. First, a person must be declared "venerable," worthy of veneration. Second, a person must be beatified, that is, declared to be in heaven and living in the presence of God. And the third stage is canonization. Around three thousand people have been canonized, many of them martyrs who died a heroic death. Only the Pope can declare a person to be a saint.

The cult of the saints was discontinued at the time of the Reformation. None of the heroes of the Reformation are regarded as saints, though some of them lived lives as exemplary and heroical as any of those previously canonized. Lutherans have a record of inconsistency on the matter of saints. Lutherans have followed the Catholic tradition in referring to some persons as saints in New Testament times and in church history. Lutheran congregations are often named after a saint, from St. Paul to St. Olaf. We have no problem referring to important figures in church history as saints, for example, St. Augustine, St. Thomas, St. Francis, and so forth. Yet, Lutherans are like other Protestants in not making much of the saints in their liturgical practices. They do not pray to saints to intercede for them. They do not venerate the saints. Some Protestants accuse Catholics of worshipping the saints, which of course is contrary to Catholic doctrine. Catholics may venerate the saints but not worship them. Neither the idea of veneration nor prayer to the saints is the same thing as worship. Not even Mary, the Mother of God, is properly the object of worship, according to Catholic dogma. It is normal for all Christians to ask others, living members of the church militant, to pray for them. Why should it be abnormal to ask those who are alive in the "church triumphant" to pray for us who are still part of the "church militant"? If we are free to ask our mother who is alive on earth to pray for us, what prevents us from asking Mary, the Mother of God, who is alive in heaven to pray for us? The New Testament teaches very clearly that nothing, not even death, "will be able to separate us from the love of God in Christ Jesus our Lord."[46]

Still, however, the dogmas regarding the Immaculate Conception and the Bodily Assumption of Mary — both of which lack biblical support — tend to elevate Mary to a status beyond humanity, approximating divinity. In Lutheran theology the term "saint" is used to refer to all believers, clearly based on New Testament precedent. Lutherans do not believe there are two separate lists of believers, those who are saints and those who are sinners. No saint on earth is born without sin, not even Mary, the Mother of Jesus. The Roman Catholic dogma of the Immaculate Conception affirms that Mary, unlike the entire human race, was not conceived in sin. She remained forever a virgin. Yet, the Gospels refer to Jesus' brothers. Supposedly Mary lived a perfect life free of all personal sin. The dogma of the Bodily Assumption of Mary affirms that Mary was assumed into heaven while still alive, bypassing death, because death is the wages of sin. If Mary is to serve as an example and model of the Christian life, it is hard to see why she should be made an exception to the whole human race, why she should be placed beyond the pale of ambiguity in which all other Christians must live by the grace of God and the forgiveness of sins. Some who wish to introduce a feminine principle into the Godhead propose the divinization of Mary, transforming the Trinity into a Quaternity. Mariology is one of those sticking points that remains unresolved in the ecumenical dialogues between churches.

What then does it means to confess that the church of sinners is indeed holy? The idea of the "holy" in the Bible is not in the first place a moral or ethical concept. The biblical concept of "holy" means to be chosen by God, to be set apart as an instrument for his special service. Holiness is not a quality that an individual possesses; it is a position in which a person stands as one chosen and set apart for service. It is positional, not possessional. As believers we cannot boast that we are holy in a moral sense. We can thank God that we have been called by the Holy Spirit to believe in Jesus as Lord and to become a member of his body, the church. Holiness is an attribute of God, first and foremost. We cannot become holy by our own reason or strength. Through repentance and faith sinful believers become participants in the holiness and righteousness of God in Christ. God looks upon the church of sinners as holy on account of Christ's saving benefits through his death and resurrection.

To be set apart does not mean to withdraw from the sinful world. We can no more leave the world behind than we can jump out of our skin. St. Simeon Stylites in the fifth century was the most extreme example of ascetic withdrawal from the world. He went into the desert and lived on top of a pillar for 36 years. Somehow he misinterpreted the message of Paul. Paul used the prepositions "in" and "of." As believers in Christ we are to live "in" the world but not "of" the world. We are called to be set apart from the worldliness of the world. Paul said it best, "Do not be conformed to this world but be transformed by the renewal of your mind, that you may prove what is the will of God, what is good and acceptable and perfect."[47]

Since the church has only sinners for its members, it would be strange if there were not a lot to criticize. There has never been a time when people did not have a long shopping list of things to complain about the church. It may be what's going on at the bureaucratic headquarters with their self-aggrandizing agendas, it may be the rigged church-wide assemblies, it may be the bishops who strut around with their pectoral crosses and purple rabats, it may be the pastors who can't preach their way out of a paper bag, it may be the seminary professors who are out of touch with the real world. It is always open season on the church, such an easy target.

The church has weathered many storms, threatened by external enemies or internal corruption, in its two millennia of history. At times of persecution it has seemed as though the church has been virtually wiped out. This happened in ancient times by the pagan Roman emperors and it happened in modern times under the communist regimes in Russia and China. Empires and nations have come and gone, but the church has survived them all. So when we think the church may be all washed up, we need to remember the words of Jesus, "Lo, I am with you always, to the close of the age."[48] God will ensure that the church will endure. By the grace of God the church will never cease to be what it is: the communion of saints, the people of God, the body of Christ, the temple of the Holy Spirit. I like this wise saying of G. K. Chesterton: "At least five times the faith has to all appearances gone to the dogs. In each of these five cases, it was the dog that died."

The church of Christ is catholic. "Catholic" means universal. The word was first applied to the church by Ignatius of Antioch around the end of the first century. He said, "Wherever the bishop is, there his people should be, just as, where Jesus Christ is, there is the Catholic Church." The meaning is that the Catholic Church is the whole church spread out around the world. In time "Catholic" took on the meaning of "orthodox," to exclude heretics and schismatics. The Roman Catholic Church claims to be the only truly catholic church. All the rest are called "separated brethren" and are accorded the status of "ecclesial communities."[49] To prove that it is the true church, Catholics are wont to claim that they are numerically the largest church on earth; they cover the whole earth and they have existed in undisrupted continuity with the church of the apostles. The Roman Catholic Church claims to be the only truly orthodox church, in that they uphold what has been believed "everywhere, always, and by all,"[50] a phrase known as the Vincentian Canon.

Such an attitude bears all the marks of the kind of self-congratulatory exaggerations that a myriad of sects assert about themselves. When a particular church claims that it is the only church that guarantees salvation,[51] that reeks with group egoism totally unbecoming a community whose Lord is Jesus Christ. It may be comforting to know that one belongs to the oldest, biggest, and most inclusive church on earth, but that does not prove it is superior to all others. Catholic polemicists use the idea of catholicity in space, time, and numbers to distinguish themselves from the hundreds of denominations and sects named after some human founder or according to a particular distinguishing characteristic. The Lutheran church is named after Luther, against his will. The Episcopal, Presbyterian, and Congregational Churches are named by their different polities, designed by the leaders who founded them. Protestants do not wish to hear that they belong to man-made organizations, not universal but regional, not numerically very large, and only of recent vintage. Lutherans number around seventy million people, named after a German monk, living mostly in Europe and America, and less than five hundred years old. Other denominations do not fare any better in terms of this idea of catholicity of space, time, and numbers. If we should enter the contest for denominational bragging rights, we are bound to lose.

However, from the perspective of Luther and the Reformation, there is no point in boasting about a church that covers the most ground, has the largest membership, the longest history, and the widest variety of cultures, if it proves to be unfaithful to the gospel and untrue to the Scriptures. To be catholic is not a quantitative thing, a mere matter of statistics, but a qualitative thing, being true and faithful to the apostolic identity and mission of the church that Jesus founded.

Confessional Lutherans do not claim to be the one and only true church.[52] They do claim to belong to the church catholic. Nathan Söderblom (1866-1931), Archbishop of Uppsala in the Church of Sweden, said that there are three great blocs of world Christianity, the Eastern Catholics we usually call the Orthodox, the Roman Catholics, and then the Evangelical Catholics, the heirs of the Reformation. Not one of the three can claim to be the whole. The Roman Catholic Church is geographically most widespread, numerically the largest, ethnically the most diverse, but that does not make it more catholic than the others. For Lutherans what makes a church catholic is primarily that it remains faithful to its apostolic origins.

The one, holy, catholic church is apostolic. The apostolicity of the church refers to the church that Jesus founded on the apostles, with himself its chief cornerstone. The apostolic church handed on down to us six inalienable characteristics that have belonged to the church from the beginning until now. We will use some familiar Greek words to identify them: *kerygma, martyria, didache, koinonia, diakonia,* and *leiturgia.* From the apostles the historic church has received the *kerygma,* the message of and about Jesus the Christ. The apostles gave us their testimony, their witness to Christ, their *martyria.* They were martyrs for Christ, because of the witness they bore to him. We have received their *didache,* the teaching of the apostles. We have been included in their *koinonia,* the fellowship of saints through prayer and the breaking of bread. For the apostles *diakonia* is a fundamental part of the Christian life, the caring ministry to the poor and the oppressed. And finally the apostles assembled the believers in Christ for *leiturgia,* for public acts of prayer, praise, and thanksgiving. It is the work of the people of God, their liturgy. We have received all these foundational things from the apostolic church.

One important feature of apostolicity remains to be discussed. That is *exousia* — the authority invested in the person of Christ and then given by him to his disciples and then the apostles. This authority did not end with the death of the last apostle. It continued to be imparted to the ongoing community through a succession of apostolic leaders by means of prayer and the laying on of hands, as recounted in the Pastoral Epistles (Titus, I & II Timothy). This was the way teaching authority was established in the early church. The writings of the apostles possessed authority. The decrees of the councils of the church possessed authority. Presbyters and bishops were endowed with authority to lead their churches and congregations. According to the apostolic tradition the authority of Christ is bestowed on those called by the Spirit into the service of the church by means of the sacrament of ordination through the imposition of hands and prayer. This is not merely the doing of human beings. It is not merely a dispensable church ceremony. It is an act of God, or it is not worth doing at all.

Apostolicity is a mark of continuity with the apostolic origins of the church. For continuity to succeed, there must be signs of succession. The core of apostolicity is the witness of

86

the apostles to Christ, given to us in the New Testament. The apostolic church led by the Spirit developed links to the future of the church in history until the end of time — signs and structures that ensure faithful continuity with the apostolic foundations of the church. To confess the apostolicity of the church without concrete visible signs and instruments of continuity is docetic. Its home base is gnosticism. Gnosticism maintains that we can dredge up the knowledge of Christ out of our own spiritual experiences.

Protestant churches today face a crisis of teaching authority. Lutheran churches seem to be in the same fix. They do not know how to deal with heresy. Bishops, pastors, and professors teach whatever they want with no worry about discipline. Dietrich Bonhoeffer wrote: "The concept of heresy has been lost today because there is no teaching authority."[53] He did not mean that we no longer accept the authority of the Bible. He did not mean that we reject the creeds of the ancient church. What Bonhoeffer possibly had in mind was that these are paper authorities. They can be ignored or twisted to mean whatever one chooses. Bonhoeffer observed that we have no living magisterium, no concrete official and public locus of authority whose task is to implement the normative sources of the Christian faith. Where does the buck stop when it comes to matters of interpretation and discipline?

The mark of apostolicity is the weak link in Lutheran ecclesiology. We have the apostolic canon, the apostolic creed, ministers and congregations where the word is preached and the sacraments are administered. Some think that is good enough. Well, it was not good enough for the ancient church. Nor was it enough for the first Lutherans, otherwise they would not have turned princes into emergency bishops. Traditionally Lutherans have rightly stressed orthodox faith; Catholics have stressed episcopal order. My view is — to paraphrase Immanuel Kant — that orthodoxy without episcopacy is blind; episcopacy without orthodoxy is empty.

Our ecumenical hope is that Lutherans will continue to work toward rapprochement with Roman Catholic and Orthodox

Churches, with the clear goal of attaining a eucharistic fellow-ship in a communion of churches. Pope John Paul II stated that "the church must once again learn to breathe with its two lungs – the Eastern and the Western one." When the schism of 1054 A. D. is overcome between the Roman Catholic Church and the Orthodox Churches, the road will be paved for Lutherans to follow suit. The Orthodox do not reject the papal office *per se*, but they cannot accept its claim to univer-sal jurisdiction. And neither can Lutherans. A reunited church of the future will surely include the primatial ministry of the papacy, but most certainly under new conditions. If Lutherans choose to remain cut off from the Catholic and Orthodox tra-ditions of doctrine, worship, spirituality, and church life, they will eventually be engulfed by the surrounding neo-pagan cul-ture now over-taking both the Liberal and Evangelical forms of Protestantism. The "Joint Declaration on the Doctrine of Justification" accepted by the Lutheran World Federation and the Vatican Congregation for the Doctrine of the Faith is a step in the right direction.

Martin Luther's Seven Marks of the Church

Martin Luther wrote an important treatise "On the Councils and the Church"[54] to answer the question how a poor con-fused person can tell where in the world the holy catholic church can be found. What are its distinguishing characteristics? Of course, he agreed with the four classical attributes of the church, that it is one, holy, catholic, and apostolic. But how can an ordinary person tell just where such a church is? He listed seven marks of the church.

1. The church is where true preaching of the Word of God takes place. This is the external word (*verbum externum*) pro-claimed in audible words that people can hear, believe, profess, and obey. If there is a group of people who regularly gather around the preaching of God's Word, that is a sure sign of a real church.

2. The second mark of recognition is the sacrament of bap-tism, wherever it is taught, believed, and administered accord-

ing to Christ's command. Wherever you see this sign, you may know that the church of Christ is surely present. It does not even matter who performs the baptism, because baptism does not belong to the baptizer. Any lay person can baptize, if it is done with the intention to act in behalf of the church.

3. The third distinguishing mark is the sacrament of the altar, wherever it is rightly administered, believed, and received according to Christ's institution. We need not worry about whether the person who administers the sacrament is worthy and holy. Some churches practice closed communion. Only communicant members of their church body may participate and only ordained pastors of that church may administer communion. Other churches practice open communion. Any person who believes in Christ and is baptized is welcomed to the Table. One of my teachers at Heidelberg University, Professor Edmund Schlink, counseled: Remember, it is the Lord's Supper, not the Church's Supper.[55] The Lord of the Church is the host who presides at his Table. It is unseemly for pastors to act like police standing at the rail separating the sheep from the goats.

4. The fourth mark is the office of the keys. The expression, "office of the keys," comes from Jesus' words to Peter, "I will give you the keys of the kingdom of heaven, and whatever you bind on earth shall be bound in heaven, and whatever you loose on earth shall be loosed in heaven."[56] Traditionally the church has practiced public and private absolution. Absolution is the act of declaring God's promise of forgiveness after confession of sin. Most churches have retained the rite of public confession and absolution, but have pretty much discontinued the practice of private confession, even among Roman Catholics. Every so often someone will mount a campaign to restore the practice of private confession, but usually it peters out. Pastoral counseling has taken its place. Among all the marks of the church, this one remains shrouded in ambiguity. Persons who confess their sins expect that the confessor will keep what he or she hears in absolute confidence. But that doesn't always happen. Some stories are just too juicy to keep

to oneself. "Don't tell anyone what I am about to tell you." And that's the start of another rumor flying around the parish. Among all the marks of the church, this one must be in search of reform and renewal.

5. The fifth mark of a real church is that it calls and ordains persons to the office of the ministry. "There must be bishops, pastors, preachers, or priests," Luther wrote, "who publicly ... administer the ... four things we have mentioned in the name of the church."[57] Not everyone in the church is called to the same vocation. Paul wrote that some are called to be apostles, some prophets, some evangelists, some teachers, and some administrators.[58] Not everyone can do all of these things. In a congregation one is called to preach, baptize, preside at the Lord's Supper, and pronounce absolution. Luther opined that if everyone would extend their hands to baptize the baby, the baby would drown. But what if one doesn't like the pastor? Luther counseled that as long as the pastor adheres to correct doctrine and practice, tolerance should prevail. But if pastors get involved in open vices, they should be removed from office.

6. The sixth mark is the assembly of people for worship, prayer, praise, and thanksgiving. In worship we pray the *Lord's Prayer* and the *Psalms*. We confess the Creed and sing hymns. We hear the reading of Scripture and the preaching of the Word. Wherever this happens, be assured that the holy people of God are present.

7. The seventh mark is bearing the cross of Christ. Those who steadfastly adhere to Christ will suffer. Jesus said, "Blessed are you when people persecute you on my account."[59] The church is built on the blood of the martyrs. Bonhoeffer called this "the cost of discipleship." Discipleship is related to the word discipline. Disciples are disciplined people.

Those are the seven marks of the church. For Luther they serve as a kind of litmus test that any poor soul can apply to any congregation. Does this congregation measure up? Does it meet the test? Every lay person must decide for his or her family.

Five Models of the Church

Jesuit priest, cardinal, and theologian, Avery Dulles (1918-2008), wrote a book on "Models of the Church." In it he described in detail five main models: 1) the church as institution, 2) the church as mystical communion, 3) the church as sacrament, 4) the church as herald, and 5) the church as servant. They do not exactly overlap Luther's seven marks of the church, but they do in part. Every church tradition is known for some particular emphasis. It may have one strong suit and be weak in others.

The church as *institution* is the strong suit of the Roman Catholic Church. Luther stated that a church must have an ordained clergy to administer its affairs in the public domain. The Roman Catholic Church is a visible institution with a complex hierarchical organization, shaped like a pyramid. The Pope presides at the top, with his seventy Cardinals. Next in line are the Archbishops, then Bishops, Priests, and Laity at the bottom. The higher the office, the bigger the hat. All power is concentrated in the hands of the properly ordained church officials. They have the authority and power to open and shut the gates of heaven. They hold the keys of the kingdom.

The church as *mystical communion* is a fellowship of people united by their common life in the Spirit. This type of church is the polar opposite of the institutional model. Here the people are bonded together in a cozy network of interpersonal relationships, sharing a life of mutual friendship and assistance. Some people join a congregation, not necessarily because it exhibits Luther's seven marks, but because the members are warm and friendly and the bathrooms are conveniently located. This is the free church tradition of independent congregations. They do not ordain their professional leaders; rather they install their charismatic leaders. Ordination is considered a Catholic concept and practice that the Reformation failed to eradicate.

3) A third model is the church as *sacrament.* The church is a sign and instrument of God's grace in the world. In its classical Augustinian tradition a sacrament is "a visible sign of an

invisible grace." The primary business of the church is to dispense the grace of God. That is what people need the most and that is why people attend a sacramental church. A sacrament is not merely an individual transaction. It is a communal event. A stranger in a foreign land may go to great lengths to find a church that offers Holy Communion. What counts is the reception of God's absolving grace and not getting a warm fuzzy experience.

4. Avery Dulles' fourth model is the church as *herald*. This is the church with which most Protestants in the Reformation tradition are familiar. The church is centered in the preaching of the gospel. The preached Word of God is two-sided. The one side is the law, the word of God's judgment and damnation; the other side is the gospel, the word of divine forgiveness and acceptance. The majority of call committees in Protestant congregations are looking for a good preacher, someone with beautiful feet, for it says in Romans, "How beautiful are the feet of those who preach good news."[60] This type of church is strong on words, often to the neglect of action. Historically, it has proved to be quietistic, not much involved in social action or prophetic protest, to improve the conditions of life for everyone, especially for those at the bottom.

5. The fifth model is the church as *servant*. Jesus is pictured as the "Man for others" and his people as the "community for others." Just as Christ came into the world to serve and not to be served, so the church is called to be Christ-like, to serve the world. This type of church is activistic, the opposite of quietistic. The church takes active stands in the interest of peace, justice, solidarity, and freedom. The weakness of this diaconal model is that it tends to neglect what is most distinctive about the church, namely, its message of the gospel, its worship of God, and its evangelistic witness to the nations. God, Christ, and the gospel of salvation are not necessary to get people to join the struggles for peace, justice, and liberty. The United Nations Declaration of Human Rights is affirmed by Hindus, Buddhists, Muslims, and Christians, val-

ues they can all share without any appeal to the Bible or the gospel of Christ. This does not mean that Christians are not to support human rights, but it does mean there is nothing exclusively Christian in doing so.

We can learn three things from Avery Dulles' typology. First, not one of these models exists in pure form. One denomination may have a strong sacramental tradition, but it may also place a high premium on good preaching. Its members may also be involved in doing community service, sponsoring food kitchens and shelters for the homeless.

Second, every church tradition, no matter what its strength, has much to learn from others. This is one of the blessings of the ecumenical movement. Through dialogue church traditions may discover beliefs and practices they have neglected due to untoward circumstances of history. A church may learn that celebrating Holy Communion only once or twice a month is a departure from the classical Christian tradition. In the ancient church the Lord's Supper was celebrated at every service on the Lord's Day. Both the ecumenical movement and the liturgical movement have had an enormous impact for change in parish ministry and congregational life.

Third, as heirs of the Reformation we realize that change is not optional. The church that lives in history must always be renewed and reformed. *Ecclesia semper reformanda* is a Latin slogan in both the Lutheran and Reformed traditions. We cannot be true to the Reformation if we cling uncritically to tradition, right or wrong. Jaroslav Pelikan coined the wise saying, "Tradition is the living faith of the dead; traditionalism is the dead faith of the living."[61] No single denomination fully embodies the great tradition of historic Christianity. There is no such thing as a perfect church. We are free to work for a robust and imaginative integration of all five models. If the best insights of each of the models are integrated and preserved in an ecumenical vision of the church, we will be moving toward a greater realization of our belief in the one, holy, catholic, and apostolic church.

Chapter Three
Ecumenism

The ecumenical goal of attaining full visible church unity has yielded to the more modest one of achieving full communion. All churches confess that the oneness of the church of Jesus Christ is one of its fundamental attributes, yet in reality they suffer the pain and humiliation of their divisions. At the beginning of the twentieth century many churches recognized that their divisions contradict the prayer of Jesus that "they may all be one ... so that the world may believe."[62] Representatives of Protestant denominations and missionary societies met in Edinburgh, Scotland, in 1910 and set as their goal, "the evangelization of the world in this generation." They realized that by continuing to slander and compete with each other, that could not be accomplished. The establishment of the World Council of Churches (WCC) in 1948 gave a tremendous impetus to the vision of Christian unity. According to its constitution the purpose of the WCC is "to call the churches to the goal of visible unity in one faith and in one eucharistic fellowship." And again they declared that unity was "in order that the world may believe."

A Vision of Christian Unity

When the Roman Catholic Church entered the ecumenical movement after the Second Vatican Council, the hopes and dreams for Christian unity seemed to stand a good chance of being realized. Many of us experienced the euphoric phase of the movement that engaged many of the best theologians in dialogue to overcome basic differences and to search for common ground. Numerous bilateral dialogues were started by the Roman Catholic Church. Anglican, Lutheran, and Reformed Churches were not far behind. From a human point of view the quest for greater Christian unity in the last 50 years must be deemed a remarkable success. Separated churches do not speak ill of each other like they used to do. Reformation Day celebrations occasionally become ecumenical events. A Catholic priest may be asked to preach. Most Christians no longer regard each other as strangers or enemies, but rather as brothers and sisters who belong to the same Christian family, however dysfunctional it may sometimes appear to be. The president of the Lutheran Church–Missouri Synod was criticized by some old-guard conservatives for writing a letter to the Pope, signing it, "Your brother in Christ." Their complaint was that the Lutheran Confessions denounce the Pope in no uncertain terms as the "Anti-Christ."

The Evangelical Lutheran Church in America has entered into full communion partnership with most of the mainline Protestant denominations — Presbyterian Church USA, Reformed Church in America, United Church of Christ, the Episcopal Church USA, the Moravian Church, and the United Methodist Church. Their full communion agreements allow for joint worship, exchange of clergy, commitment to shared evangelism, witness and service in the world. The ELCA bases its ecumenical policy on Article VII of the *Augsburg Confession* which states that "it is enough for the true unity of the church to agree concerning the teaching of the gospel and the administration of the sacraments." The theological question still remains open, however. Do all these churches share a common confession of the Christian faith? Saying so doesn't make it so. Do they actually agree on the essentials of the gospel? Do they all believe, for example, in the real presence of Christ "in, with, and under" the sacramental elements of bread and wine? Opinion polls indicate that most of the Protestants in North America are positively Zwinglian in their theology of

96

the Lord's Supper. Moreover, a majority vote at a churchwide convention cast by members who lack the theological acumen to grasp what they are voting on must give one pause. The most disconcerting explanation for the ease with which the ELCA was able to reach full communion agreements with six denominations in North America is the fact that it has increasingly become more Protestant in its self-understanding and less Catholic. I regard this trend as lamentable and a travesty of the catholicity of the confessional heritage of the Lutheran Reformation.

Lutheran-Roman Catholic Dialogues

Lutheran and Catholic theologians have been engaged in dialogue since 1965 when the Vatican and the Lutheran World Federation agreed to form a working group with the manifest purpose to seek greater unity in the truth of the gospel, to remove historic differences that have divided their two communions, and to make progress toward full visible church unity. Two sets of Lutheran-Roman Catholic dialogues have taken place, one at the international level and the other in the United States. Their combined output has been massive in scope and profound in scholarship. They prove that what unites Lutherans and Catholics is much greater than what separates them. In these dialogues Lutherans have shown their catholic face and Catholics have shown their evangelical face. As a result their ecumenical potential for realizing their unity in Christ is incalculably great. The participating theologians have done their work with a remarkable degree of success. That has been matched by utter failure on the part of church officials to take the necessary steps to receive and implement whatever agreements have been reached. This failure is especially regrettable with respect to the *Joint Declaration on the Doctrine of Justification*, signed by the Lutheran World Federation and the Vatican Pontifical Council for Promoting Christian Unity. What changes at the parish or diocesan levels has their professed consensus on basic truths of the gospel brought about? It's as though two persons agree to marry and then fail to go to the altar. If there is agreement in theory on justification — the article by which the church stands and falls — and that agreement makes no practical difference, say, at the Lord's Table, then the document is hardly worth the paper it's printed on.

The USA Lutheran-Catholic Dialogues have published common statements and background papers on eleven different topics. Having read, analyzed, and evaluated all of them, I have concluded that there is only one church-dividing issue that remains on the table; that is the dogma of papal infallibility and its claim to universal jurisdiction. On all the other topics, the theological differences within each of the two church traditions is as great as those between them. In my judgment such differences need not keep the churches from expressing their shared unity in Christ where it matters the most, at the Table of the Lord. The first dialogue (1965) dealt with "The Status of the Nicene Creed as Dogma of the Church." The function of this Creed was to outlaw the Arian heresy that denies the divinity of Christ and renders him a semi-divine creature. The truth of this dogma derives from Scripture and is taught on the authority of the church. On this Lutherans and Catholics agree, in the face of colossal modern Protestant apostasy — from Schleiermacher to Ritschl in the nineteenth century as well as process (Schubert Ogden, David Griffin, and others) and feminist theologians in the twentieth century (Carter Heyward, Sallie McFague, and others) — that welcome Arian teaching back into the fold.

The second dialogue was on the topic of "One Baptism for the Remission of Sins" (1967). One would not expect any church-dividing disagreements on baptism, and that was borne out by the concluding "Joint Statement": "We were reasonably certain that the teachings of our respective traditions regarding baptism are in substantial agreement, and this opinion has been confirmed at this meeting."

The third dialogue dealt with "The Eucharist as Sacrifice." Here a Lutheran might anticipate some difficulty. Traditionally Lutherans have not called the Sacrament of the Altar "the Eucharist." Eucharist means "thanksgiving," and that is something Christians do from their side. For Lutherans Holy Communion is primarily something God does from his side. He grants the forgiveness of sins, life, and salvation, gifts which we receive and for which we respond with our praise and thanksgiving.

There are two kinds of sacrifice. The one is the *atoning* sacrifice of Christ on the cross that reconciles us to God. The other is the *eucharistic* sacrifice by which we give thanks to God for the forgiveness of sins.[63] Only the death of Christ is atoning; there is no need for any additional sacrifice. The eucharistic sacrifices of prayer, praise, and thanksgiving of the worshipping community do not work reconciliation or merit forgiveness. Of course, Lutherans believe in the eucharist as sacrifice — as something we do in Holy Communion again and again. The atoning sacrifice of Christ on the cross is a finished work, done once for all and does not need to be repeated. Such, I believe, is the traditional Lutheran understanding of sacrament and sacrifice. Now, let us see what our Lutheran and Catholic dialogue partners came up with.

They came to a mutual understanding that Catholics as well as Lutherans affirm the once-for-all character and full sufficiency of Christ's sacrifice on the cross. Lutherans have feared that Catholics teach that the sacrifice of Christ is repeated in the Eucharist. This is not what Catholics intend to say. Catholics clarified that what they mean is not repetition but re-presentation, not doing the sacrifice over again but making the once-for-all event of salvation present again and again.

Catholics have often lumped Lutherans together with the Reformed Protestants for whom the Lord's Supper is primarily a memorial of Christ's death on the cross. In this view Christ may be said to be spiritually present, symbolized by the bread and the wine. Lutherans teach that the crucified and risen Lord is wholly, truly, and personally present in both his human and divine natures in, with, and under the bread and wine. Catholics thought that for Lutherans like for the Reformed the presence of Christ is somehow dependent on the faith of the recipient, whereas Lutherans believe that the whole Christ is really present by virtue of the dominical words of institution, before, during, and after the eating and drinking. Thus their common statement affirms that both Catholics and Lutherans believe in the "real presence" of Christ, and they distinguish it from a purely commemorative understanding of the sacrament. Does that mean they agree on everything? By no means. Traditionally they use different terminology to express and explain what is happening in the sacrament. But they do agree on what is essential. The full reality of Christ is present in the sacrament of the altar. In my view, their remaining disagreements do not rise to the level of necessarily excluding each other from a common celebration of the Lord's Supper. The continuing practice of "closed communion" must rest on grounds other than disagreements on the Lord's Supper.

The fourth dialogue in the series dealt with "Eucharist and Ministry." Are there church-dividing differences on the proper administration of Holy Communion? Who is competent to preside at the celebration of the Lord's Supper? The problem of the ministry had to be treated head on, because it tends to hang over every dialogue like a dark cloud. Both sides agreed that the special ministry of the church must be treated within the context of the general ministry of the whole people of God. The contentious issues have to do with the meaning of "apostolic succession" and "ordination." For Catholics apostolic succession refers to an unbroken chain of sacramental acts of ordination through prayer and the laying on of hands, linking today's priests with the apostles of Jesus. For Lutherans apostolic succession has meant primarily ongoing faithfulness to apostolic faith and doctrine. Study of the church fathers indicates that the two emphases are not mutually exclusive. The primary purpose of succession in the apostolic office is to ensure succession in the apostolic faith and doctrine.

For both Catholics and Lutherans ordination is the means of entry into the special ministry of the church. For Catholics ordination is a sacrament. Lutherans have been reluctant to call it a sacrament, although the *Apology of the Augsburg Confession* allows for it. What's in a name? Functionally speaking ordination means the same thing in both traditions. The act of ordination is a sign that a person is set apart for service in and for the church. It is performed by invoking the Holy Spirit to bestow a gift — a charism — for ministry, accompanied by prayer and the laying on of hands by someone already ordained.

Ordination is done once-for-all. In neither tradition is it meant to be repeated. The fact that re-ordination is practiced by either church is a sign that something is broken — the church is suffering the scandal of disunity. To emphasize the quality of permanence Catholics have used the term "*character indelebilis*," a term absent from Lutheran vocabulary. However, Lutherans too stress the indelible character of ordination as a divine calling enacted by the church for life-long service. Ordained ministers may betray their calling, stray into heresy, and even commit apostasy, but they can never remove the mark the Spirit has etched upon their souls for service in Christ's church.

The outcome of these exchanges between Catholic and Lutheran theologians on the doctrine of the ministry is unprecedented and far-reaching. The Lutherans affirmed the following: "As Lutherans, we joyfully witness that in theological dialogue with our Roman Catholic partners we have again seen clearly a fidelity to the proclamation of the gospel and the administration of the sacraments which confirms our historic conviction that the Roman Catholic Church is an authentic church of our Lord Jesus Christ. For this reason we recommend to those who have appointed us that through appropriate channels the participating Lutheran churches be urged to declare formally their judgment that the ordained Ministers of the Roman Catholic Church are engaged in a valid Ministry of the gospel, announcing the gospel of Christ and administering the sacraments of faith as their chief responsibilities, and that the body and blood of our Lord Jesus Christ are truly present in their celebrations of the sacrament of the altar."[64]

The Roman Catholic participants responded in the same spirit of commendation. "As Roman Catholic theologians, we acknowledge in the spirit of Vatican II that the Lutheran communities with which we have been in dialogue are truly Christian churches, possessing the elements of holiness and truth that mark them as organs of grace and salvation. Furthermore, in our study we have found serious defects in the arguments customarily used against the validity of the eucharistic Ministry of the Lutheran churches. In fact, we see no persuasive reason to deny the possibility of the Roman Catholic church recognizing the validity of this Ministry. Accordingly we ask the authorities of the Roman Catholic church whether the ecumenical urgency flowing from Christ's will for unity may not dictate that the Roman Catholic church recognize the validity of the Lutheran Ministry and, correspondingly, the presence of the body and blood of Christ in the eucharistic celebrations of the Lutheran churches."[65]

The theologians did their work in removing obstacles that have traditionally kept Lutherans and Catholics communing at separate altars. Their respective judicatories did nothing to receive and act on their statements and requests.

The fifth and sixth dialogues dealt with what has ecumenically come to be known as "the big elephant in the room." The fifth dealt with papal primacy and the sixth with papal infallibility. The two topics should not be conflated. Theologically it is not at all inconsistent to be in favor of papal primacy and to be against papal infallibility. In fact, that is how I have understood the confessional Lutheran position since I began thinking and writing on structures of governance and authority in the church. The Lutheran and Catholic theologians in this fifth dialogue issued a common statement in which they expressed a consensus on a number of traditionally controversial topics. Lutherans are increasingly aware of the necessity of a specific Ministry to serve the church's unity and universal mission. Catholics see the need for rethinking the role of the papacy within the universal church.[66] Just as a pastor is called and ordained to a position of primacy within a local congregation, and a bishop likewise is ordained and installed into a position of primacy in a particular diocese or synod, so there can hardly be any reasonable objection to having a Ministry of primacy in the one universal church on earth. Papal primacy is therefore acceptable provided it is so structured as to serve the gospel and the unity of the church of Christ.

In light of the agreements that these theologians reached, they asked their respective churches to take specific actions toward reconciliation. If papal primacy is no longer a barrier to reconciliation, what would such reconciliation entail? It would mean that Lutherans accept the teaching Ministry of the Pope not only for Roman Catholics, but also for Lutherans. This is already happening to the extent that Lutheran theologians take seriously the many papal encyclicals that have been promulgated since Vatican II. One could say without exaggeration that the recent popes, for example, John XXIII, John Paul II and Benedict XVI, have proved to be more faithful teachers of the biblical message and church doctrine than bishops and theologians of the mainline Protestant churches.

Reconciliation would also mean that the legitimate substance of the Lutheran confessional tradition and spiritual heritage would be respected, allowing for self-government of Lutheran churches within a communion of churches. Lutherans would not be required to surrender their Lutheran identity anymore than Jesuits, Dominicans, or Benedictines are asked to relinquish their distinctive heritages by their association with the Bishop of Rome. Lutheran churches would be accepted as sister-churches in a communion of churches. That is the vision. One baby step toward its realization was taken when the Vatican Pontifical Council for Promoting Christian Unity and the Lutheran World Federation signed the *Joint Declaration on the Doctrine of Justification by Faith.* The implications of this confession for reconciliation and inter-communion remain to be thought through and implemented step-by-step in the decades and centuries to come. Meanwhile we press forward in hope and prayer that the Ministry of Christ's Church at the local, regional, and universal levels will become truly evangelical, renewed according to the gospel. The Joint Declaration calls for nothing less.

Throughout the fifth dialogue on papal primacy the theologians kept referring to a big bogeyman lurking down the road, the doctrine of papal infallibility. Agreement on papal primacy to meet the need for a Ministry that serves the universal Church would include acknowledgment of its authority, but not necessarily one that is infallible. Primacy is one thing, infallibility another. Nevertheless, the Lutherans in this sixth dialogue met their Catholic partners halfway in imagining new ways to interpret the dogma of papal infallibility in a more favorable light, and therefore no longer *ipso facto* an insuperable barrier to reconciliation and the unity of the churches.

The word "infallibility" is nowhere to be found in the Scriptures and was only applied to the church's teaching authority in the fourteenth century.[67] The intention was a good one — to emphasize the faithful transmission of the gospel and its authoritative interpretation by the church, under the guidance of the Holy Spirit. Thus, Lutherans and Catholics "share the certainty of Christian hope that the Church, established by Christ and led by the Spirit, will always remain in the truth fulfilling its mission to humanity for the sake of the gospel."[68] Lutherans now see that for Catholics — at least for these Catholic theologians in the dialogue — the doctrine of infallibility expresses confidence that the Spirit of God abides in his Church and will fulfill the promise of Christ to be with his Church "to the close of the age" (Matt. 28:20). While Lutherans will not use the infallibility language, they may speak of the indefectibility of the church to express their confidence that God will not permit his Church to defect from the truth indefinitely.

At the end of the dialogue Lutherans made it clear that if infallibility means inerrancy, they cannot only not affirm it of the papacy but also of no other institution, office, or doctrine of the church, not even of the Scriptures or the Creeds. Inerrancy is an attribute of the gospel of God's justifying grace in Christ to which the Scriptures bear witness and which the tradition of the church transmits by its creeds, confessions, and liturgies. However, the Lutheran theologians admitted that, despite their difficulty with talk of infallibility, they appreciate the importance of a universal teaching Ministry within the Church. Decisions about the truth of the gospel in faithfulness to Scripture must be made from time to time, as the ancient councils of the church did. To fulfill this responsibility Catholics are empowered by a *magisterium* which can articulate matters of faith and doctrine in an effective way. Lutherans around the world today have no *magisterium*. The best they can do is to listen and learn from the Catholic contributions in the areas of doctrine and ethics in the process of hammering out their own statements. If the ELCA would have done this in preparation of its "Social Statement on Human Sexuality," it might have been spared its un-ecumenical slide into the heresy of antinomianism. If Lutheranism today is to continue to be a gospel-centered reform movement within the western branch of the church catholic, it cannot allow itself to proceed in sectarian isolation without consultation with Roman Catholic theologians. Acting on such denominational independence makes a mockery of the decades of dialogue, reaching remarkable degrees of rapprochement between Lutherans and Catholics. It makes no sense for a Lutheran denomination to go it alone in an ecumenical age.

Lutherans and Catholics in the seventh dialogue finally got around to the doctrine of justification by faith. That was the logical step because in their treatment of papal infallibility Lutherans kept asserting that their difficulty with the dogma stemmed from their commitment to the primacy of the gospel of God's justifying act in Christ. If that is so, the Catholic theologians concluded: ""We, therefore, need to discuss the doctrine of justification, a doctrine at the very root of the Reformation itself."[69] And so they did.

At the conclusion of this dialogue on justification these Lutheran and Catholic theologians stunned their respective churches with the sensational declaration, "A fundamental consensus on the gospel is necessary to give credibility to our previous agreed statements on baptism, on the Eucharist, and on forms of church authority. We believe that we have reached such a consensus."[70] This statement helps to explain what they meant by consensus: "Our entire hope of justification and salvation rests on Christ Jesus and on the gospel whereby the good news of God's merciful action in Christ is made known; we do not place our ultimate trust in anything other than God's promise and saving work in Christ. This excludes ultimate reliance on our faith, virtues, or merits, even though we acknowledge God working in these by grace alone (*sola gratia*)."[71]

In historical perspective all the background work for this USA dialogue on justification paved the way for the international dialogue of Catholics and Lutherans that produced the *Joint Declaration on the Doctrine of Justification*. The strategy adopted by both dialogues was the same. When Lutherans and Catholics speak about justification, they do not mean the same thing. Martin Chemnitz made that clear in his *Examination of the Council of Trent*, written during the years 1565-1573. For Lutherans justification is the imputation of the righteousness of Christ apprehended by faith. Sanctification follows, the renewing work of the Spirit to generate love and good works. For Catholics justification is used in the broader sense to include the whole process of salvation, both the external imputation of righteousness and the internal renewal of life. Catholics have a hard time thinking about salvation as a matter of faith alone, apart from love and good works. Salvation is thought of as an ongoing process of life-long transformation. The movement is horizontal. For Lutherans the act of justification is a complete transaction descending vertically from above, actualizing the unconditional love of God through the forgiveness of sins, declaring sinners righteous solely on account of Christ. Love and good works follow from a living faith. The righteousness that counts before God is a pure gift of grace and not something acquired by human cooperation.

In the Lutheran confessional tradition the doctrine of justification has been accorded a unique place in the system of Christian doctrine (dogmatics), as the article by which the church stands and falls (*articulus stantis et cadentis ecclesiae*). For Lutherans it is *the* critical principle, norm, and standard

106

by which everything else is judged. Catholics hear Lutherans to be saying that it is the *only* critical principle, meriting the charge of gospel-reductionism. Catholic theologians are happy to say that justification is a critical principle, but not one that stands alone. There is need of a second principle, namely, the catholic substance which the Spirit of God has created in the life and history of the church, its Scriptures, Creeds, Sacraments, and Liturgies. Paul Tillich said it well when he coined the terms, "Protestant principle and Catholic substance." One without the other leads away from the fullness of the apostolic faith and doctrine of the one, holy, catholic church.

Did these Catholic and Lutheran dialogue partners really attain a fundamental consensus on the gospel, as they claimed? They submitted their findings to their respective churches for further study and testing, with the hope that appropriate decisions would be made for the sake of confessing one faith. What they suggest is that a fundamental consensus on the gospel does not call for homogenizing Lutheran and Roman Catholic theology. Two theologies may be very different from each other, without either one being unfaithful to the gospel. The history of theology shows a great variety of theologies within the framework of confessing the one faith in the conceptual categories of many creeds and confessions of the church. The doctrine of justification will never acquire the same role and significance to Catholics as it has meant to Lutherans. The same thing can be said about the Pope and Mary in relation to Lutherans. Assent to the truth of a doctrine may occur upfront with the head, and leave the heart lagging far behind — a comment that serves as a suitable segue to the next topic.

The eighth dialogue dealt with "The One Mediator, the Saints, and Mary." I have preached on Mary from the appropriate Gospel texts, and I believe I said the right things, but truth be told, my heart could not keep up with my head. Why is that? As a Lutheran raised in the tradition of pietism, we learned about Mary and Joseph and the baby Jesus, but we never prayed to Mary. She did not figure in our private devotions. Needless to say, none of the saints fared any better.

In the course of my studies I was surprised to learn that Luther had a high appreciation of Mary. He confessed that Mary was a virgin, even always a virgin (*semper virgine*), and that she is the Mother of God (*theotokos*), as also do the Lutheran Confessions. He professed his belief in the Immaculate Conception of Mary and he preached on the Assumption of Mary. Of course, he did not equate these pious beliefs with articles of faith. They lack scriptural support and are latecomers in the development of piety and dogma. The periods of orthodoxy, pietism, and rationalism took all the starch out of the high honor and devotion paid to Mary by Luther and the Lutheran Confessions.

Protestants generally over-reacted to the abuses of the cult of Mary and the Saints in Roman Catholicism to the point where any mention of them, as in liturgical commemorations, supposedly detracted from the uniqueness of Christ as the sole mediator of salvation. The *Augsburg Confession*, Article 21, states: "Saints may be remembered in order that we may imitate their faith and good works strengthened." The sad fact is that Mary and the Saints have been pretty much forgotten in Lutheran piety and worship. However, the *Lutheran Book of Worship* (LBW) made a serious effort to restore the liturgical practice of commemorating Mary and the Saints on festival occasions. How many pastors and worship leaders are engaged in this uphill effort at liturgical renewal?

Yet, in this dialogue on Mary and the Saints, our Lutheran representatives, despite their irenic spirit and ecumenical commitment, were not able to find common ground with their Roman Catholic partners on the practice of invoking Mary and the Saints to intercede for them and their departed loved ones. The crux of the Lutheran objection was, first, the sole mediatorship of Christ and, second, the lack of any biblical promise that Mary and the Saints can hear prayers and are able to help the living or the dead in their need. Saints may be beneficial models of faith in Christ but they are not mediators of special graces. Even when all the abuses have been removed, Lutherans do not see a green light, biblically and confessionally speaking, to initiate the practices of intercession and invocation of the Saints and Mary in a way that concurs with their criterion of justification by faith in Christ, the sole saving mediator between God and human beings.

Catholics respond that there is no impenetrable curtain that separates the living saints from those who have died in union with Christ. They agree that there is no direct biblical support for intercession and invocation of saints, but they believe the church has been led by the Spirit to include the dead in the biblical practice of asking members of the communion of saints to pray for each other. Catholics do not see that prayer to the triune God and invoking the Saints are mutually exclusive. It is not an either/or. The same is true about the dogmas of the Immaculate Conception and the Assumption of Mary. They may lack support in the Scriptures, but Catholics believe the Spirit has guided the church in the development of these dogmas.

Since the traditional differences could not be removed after seven years of dialogue, the question both sides faced was: are they necessarily church-dividing? Do they call into question the claim that concluded their dialogue on justification by faith that they shared a fundamental consensus on the gospel? The matters of intercession and invocation need not impede reconciliation, for this reason: the Catholic Church does not require its members to practice them. Some do and those who do not still enjoy full communion within the Catholic Church. The same freedom could be extended to Lutherans. Lutherans might consider calling them *adiaphora.* Moreover, Catholics do not understand them to detract from the unique mediatorship of Christ.

The Marian dogmas pose a greater difficulty. The consensus statement of the dialogue made a realistic assessment: "The two Marian dogmas must be acknowledged as an obstacle to full fellowship between our churches, though they need not prevent a significant advance in the relationship that already exists." Nevertheless, the dialogue made some bold suggestions about the next steps the two churches could take: 1) Lutherans could acknowledge that Catholic teaching about the Saints and Mary does not promote idolatrous belief and practice and is not opposed to the gospel. 2) Catholics could acknowledge that Lutherans would not be obliged to invoke the Saints or to affirm the two Marian dogmas.

To reach the goal of full visible unity in faith and life the divided churches will need to tolerate a great variety of worship beliefs and practices across the ecumenical spectrum. Facing Churches to the right — Catholic and Orthodox — Lutherans will need to overcome the iconoclastic tendencies acquired over time from their fellow Protestants and allow for the cult of Mary and the Saints unfamiliar to them. Facing Churches to the left — some Evangelicals and Pentecostals — Lutherans will need to have a more positive appreciation of the charismatic gifts — healing miracles, demon exorcism, and speaking in tongues. Will it be possible for churches in the future to accept such a fantastic pluralism of worship practices and still claim with integrity to share a consensus in the doctrine of the gospel, as expressed, for example, by the *Joint Declaration on the Doctrine of Justification?* The prospect is mind-boggling.

The ninth dialogue took up a topic that had been hovering like a hawk over all the conversations: Scripture and Tradition. They came to the table with the usual caricatures of each other's positions: Lutherans supposedly affirm *sola scriptura* and reject tradition. Catholics supposedly believe in two equal sources of God's revelation, one part in Scripture and the other part in tradition. They learned that they are not so different after all. Lutherans do not reject tradition, otherwise they could not subscribe to their confessional writings of the sixteenth century (the *Book of Concord*) as true witnesses to the Word of God and trustworthy summaries of the faith of the Christian Church. And they do this not merely insofar as (*quatenus*) but because (*quia*) they present and explain the pure doctrine of the gospel. Lutherans have a high doctrine of the role and significance of tradition as the cumulative history of the transmission of the church's preaching and teaching of the Word of God in Holy Scripture and rightly interpreted by the ancient Creeds of the Church. This came as a pleasant surprise to the Catholic partners in dialogue.

From their side Catholic theologians assured their Lutheran colleagues that the dogmatic treatise *Dei Verbum* of Vatican II moved away from the two-source (*partim-partim*) theory of divine revelation in Catholic neo-scholastic theology. Tradition is not a separate source of faith and doctrine on a par with Scripture. Here Lutherans were able to remind Catholics that in the early church it was the Gnostics who appealed to a special tradition not found in Scripture. The function of tradition and of the *magisterium* is rather to hand on and interpret the revelation of God in Christ attested in a definitive way by Scripture.

Differences of terminology and emphasis may well remain between Lutherans and Catholics on the relation between Scripture and tradition. Lutherans, for example, will continue to speak of *sola scriptura*, affirming Scripture as the ultimate standard by which all subsequent traditions must be judged. Catholics will answer, yes, Scripture is the decisive norm, but it is not the only norm. The apostolic tradition handed down through creeds and liturgies consistent with Scripture is also accorded normative status. Lutherans can hardly disagree, given that their own Confessions affirm the normative status of the three ancient Creeds, the Apostles', the Nicene, and the Athanasian, "as the glorious confessions of the faith — succinct, Christian, and based upon the Word of God."[72] Thus, the question is: are there still church-dividing differences? That is for the churches to decide, once they receive the findings of this dialogue. It should be remembered that it is not the purpose of ecumenical dialogues to shave away all the theological differences between ecclesial traditions, but rather to examine whether such differences present insuperable obstacles to eucharistic fellowship and church unity.

Here is a verbatim statement of the points of agreement on Scripture and Tradition at the conclusion of this dialogue.

1) Holy Scripture has preeminent status as the Word of God, committed to writing in an unalterable manner.

2) Before the Old and New Testaments existed in written form, the Word of God was carried by tradition.

3) Under the guidance of the Holy Spirit Scripture gives rise to the oral proclamation of law and gospel.

4) The preeminent status of Scripture does not preclude the function of a teaching office or the legitimacy of doctrinal traditions that protect and promote the reliance of the faithful on the gospel message of Christ and grace alone (*solus Christus* and *sola gratia*).

5) There are no historically verifiable apostolic traditions that are not attested in some way by Scripture.

6) Not all true doctrine needs to be simply and literally present in the Bible, but may be deduced from it.

7) The teaching of doctrine in the church is never above the Word of God, but must serve that Word and be in conformity with it.

The tenth dialogue finally got around to ecclesiology. Its discussions and recommendations were organized around the concept of the church as *koinonia*. The published volume is entitled "The Church as Koinonia of Salvation: Its Structures & Ministries." *Koinonia* is a New Testament word meaning "fellowship," but its use as an ecclesiological concept is of recent vintage, gaining widespread currency in post-Vatican II ecumenical literature. Two books are especially noteworthy. One is by an Orthodox theologian, John D. Zizioulas, *Being as Communion. Studies in Personhood and the Church*.[73] The other is by a Roman Catholic theologian, J.-M. R. Tillard, *Church of Churches: The Ecclesiology of Communion*."[74] *Koinonia* ecclesiology was adopted by virtually all the churches in their bi-lateral dialogues because it offers a point of departure not over-loaded with the negative history of controversy and polemic. The church as *koinonia* (in Greek) or *communio* (in Latin) expresses the nature of the church as a universal reality that exists in many local communities.

Defining the church as a communion of churches brings new perspectives to bear on a wide range of old problems.

After airing their differences the dialogue presented to the churches some audacious recommendations that are far from being received and implemented by either church body. Here are some samples.

1) "We recommend that each church recognize that the other realizes, even if perhaps imperfectly, the one church of Jesus Christ and shares in the apostolic tradition."

2) "We recommend that each church recognize that the ordained ministry of the other effectively carries on, even if perhaps imperfectly, the apostolic ministry instituted by God in the church."

3) "We recommend that Roman Catholic criteria for assessing authentic ministry include attention to a ministry's faithfulness to the gospel and its service to the communion of the church, and that the term *defectus ordinis* as applied to Lutheran ministries be translated as 'deficiency' rather than 'lack.'"

4) "We recommend that Catholics explore how the universal ministry of the bishop of Rome can be reformed to manifest more visibly its subjection to the gospel in service to the *koinonia* of salvation."

5) "We recommend that Lutherans explore whether the worldwide *koinonia* of the church calls for a worldwide minister of unity and what form such a ministry might take to be truly evangelical."

6) "We recommend that our churches recognize the real but imperfect communion among our ministers and encourage appropriate forms of pastoral collaboration between our ministries."

We have here a diplomatically worded wish list that fails to achieve a breakthrough on the historic church-dividing issues on ministry and authority in the church. The differences on ordination, succession, episcopacy, and papacy did not yield to these expert practitioners of the art of ecumenical politesse.

The eleventh round of the U.S. Lutheran-Roman Catholic dialogue took up the topic of eschatology. It is entitled, "The

Hope of Eternal Life." It is perhaps the most interesting read of all the dialogues, and I whole-heartedly recommend its use as a teaching text in parish education. The questions this dialogue attempts to answer inevitably come to the fore at every funeral. All parishioners have at least some vague and possibly strange notions, and perhaps even worries, about death and damnation, heaven and hell. Most of them will know something about the disputed issues between Lutherans and Catholics, such as purgatory, indulgences, and prayers for the dead. Traditional caricatures abound on both sides, and flourish in a context of ignorance and superstition. This dialogue treats all of the controversial issues in ways that are historically informative, thoroughly theological, and pastorally responsible.

The dialogue was wise to draw upon the prior agreement between Lutherans and Catholics, namely, *The Joint Declaration on the Doctrine of Justification*. This statement inspired and encouraged the participants to find common ground in their shared hope of eternal life on account of Jesus' resurrection from the dead. The claim of common ground does not mean that the historic differences in teaching and practice no longer exist. The dialogue is frank to state what they are. Nevertheless, the conclusion of the dialogue is bold and challenging. It states that the remaining differences between Lutherans and Catholics on indulgences, prayer for the dead, and purgation need not be church-dividing or communion-hindering. Would all Lutherans agree with that? Hardly. The representatives from the Lutheran Church–Missouri Synod said "No. More work needs to be done."

The Princeton Proposal

Twenty years ago (1991) LaVonne (my wife) and I together with Robert and Blanche Jenson founded the Center for Catholic and Evangelical Theology. Its mission statement reads as follows: "The Center for Catholic and Evangelical Theology is an ecumenical organization that seeks to cultivate faithfulness to the gospel of Jesus Christ throughout the churches. The

Center nurtures theology that is catholic and evangelical, obe-dient to Holy Scripture and committed to the dogmatic, litur-gical, ethical, and institutional continuity of the church. The Center challenges the churches to claim their identity as mem-bers of the One, Holy, Catholic and Apostolic Church. It af-firms the Great Tradition and seeks to stimulate fresh think-ing and passion for mission. To achieve this goal the Center sponsors projects, conferences, and publications."

We founded the Center because we believe that differences that continue to divide Christians and churches prevent them from giving a common witness to the gospel of Christ and working together for its global outreach. In spite of all the criti-cisms calling the modern ecumenical movement into question, the Center decided that it would be timely and useful to as-semble a group of veteran ecumenists and younger theologians to consider what might be called the ecclesiology of ecumenics. Sixteen members were invited to form the group. Since they were not chosen *by* their respective churches, they were not duty bound to speak *for* their churches. Thus they would be free to deliberate as an independent group and produce a state-ment — a manifesto — that speaks to the churches. Members came from across the ecumenical spectrum, from Pentecostal to Orthodox and in-between — Roman Catholics, Anglicans, Methodists, Reformed, and Lutheran.

The title of the document produced by this group is *In One Body through the Cross*, and its sub-title is *The Princeton Proposal for Christian Unity* (2003), named after the place where we met twice a year, three days at a time, for three and a half years. The statement was published by Wm. B. Eerdmans Publishing Company, 50 pages of text, set forth in 72 para-graphs, with seven sections. It was written and signed by the 16 members, not as fully representative of Christianity in America as would have been ideal. Though Jenson and I participated in the discussions, as moderators and finally as editors of the manifesto, we did not sign it. The experience was interesting and members of the group bonded in ways that will endure. The process we followed was to have members of the group

115

write papers on a wide variety of controversial issues, which were subsequently published by Eerdmans, entitled *The Ecumenical Future: Background Papers for the Princeton Proposal* (2004).

Rather quickly the group reached agreement on several decisive points. First, the World Council of Churches had it right at the start, at an important meeting of modern ecumenism in New Delhi in 1961. Its statement says that the unity of the church "is being made visible as all in each place who are baptized into Christ Jesus and confess him as Lord and Savior are brought by the Holy Spirit into one fully committed fellowship, holding one apostolic faith, preaching the one Gospel, breaking the one bread, joining in common prayer, and having a corporate life reaching out in witness and service to all and who at the same time are united with the whole Christian fellowship in all places and all ages, in such wise that ministry and members are accepted by all, and that all can act and speak together as occasion requires for the tasks to which God calls his people."

Second, church division, the absence of unity, has had a debilitating and enfeebling effect on the interior life of each denomination. In the judgment of the group, much of the inner turmoil and disintegration that we see in the churches is the result precisely of their separation from one another. Mission is inhibited and discredited by the church's divisions, since according to the Gospel of John, chapter 17, Jesus prayed that his disciples would be one, so that the world might believe.

Third, in our current religious and theological situation the concern for denominational identity trumps commitment to truth. One feature of living in the global village is that people become concerned about their unique personal or collective identity. The search is on everywhere for cultural, national, ethnic, and religious identity. The operative question is not: what is true or what is right or what is good? The more common question is: Who am I? Who are we? Are we being loyal to our identity inscribed in our denominational DNA? Are we

116

being faithful to our founding fathers? Are we good Lutherans? Are we good Methodists? Ecumenism can easily be viewed as a seduction that weakens or even abolishes denominational identity, resulting in a relativized pluralism and a meltdown of our cherished traditions.

The *Princeton Proposal* strongly gives priority to the matter of truth. For example, if some practice or teaching is loyal to the Lutheran tradition, that does not make it true. Lutherans love to quote Martin Luther. But *"was Luther sagt"* does not necessarily prove something is true. Everything has to be tested anew by the canons of truth incumbent upon all Christians. That is the import of the reformation slogan, *sola scriptura*. Scripture takes precedence over tradition. A particular denominational identity must not be allowed to trump universal Christian truth. Lutheran identity takes us back five centuries at the most; Anglican, Methodist, and Baptist identities even less. Christian truth takes us back to the beginnings — *ad fontes* — to the original sources of ecclesial identity in the Holy Scriptures, which cradle the truth of God's definitive revelation. When we do that we find that we can no longer be content to swim in our narrow denominational streams. We must learn to swim together with all the others in the deeper waters of Scripture as well as take into account fifteen centuries of pre-reformational classical Christian tradition, the Great Tradition that antedates our most revered Protestant traditions.

The *Princeton Proposal* stands against any easy irenicism, relativism, or indifferentism, convinced that authentic work for church unity cannot afford to disregard the truth of doctrine. If identity were the all-important concern, there would be no need for dialogue aiming to overcome church-dividing differences.

The basic idea of the *Princeton Proposal* is that Christian unity already exists in some real sense; it exists wherever Christ is present in faith itself. Union with Christ is a gift of the Holy Spirit to which we cannot add and from which we cannot subtract. Believers already experience full communion with God in Christ in the fellowship of the Holy Spirit. When we, in our separated churches, receive the body and blood of our Lord Jesus Christ, that is *koinonia,* full communion, not partial or imperfect communion. Christ cannot be divided. But the unity we share in Christ in the vertical dimension is something that members of his body should manifest in the horizontal dimension. The unity we seek in the ecumenical movement is based on the unity we have been given sacramentally in baptism. To oppose the primary goal of ecumenism is to deny that our Christian obligation is to seek unity between all churches and Christians now separated from each other. In German a distinction is made between *Gabe* and *Aufgabe,* gift and task. In English we distinguish between the theological indicative and the ethical imperative. In the language of the New Testament, faith without works is dead. Justification is the prior initiatory act of God. Sanctification is a word that describes the life that follows — the life-long pursuit of holiness.

The *Princeton Proposal* does not mince words. It calls the separation of churches a sin. Our churches have been divided so long, that division has come to appear as normal, as something we should simply accept as fixed forever. It is easy for Americans to accept it: competition is thought to be a good thing. It keeps everyone on their toes. But alas, that contradicts the picture of the church we find in the New Testament. The competition between Peter and Paul and James on law and gospel and on faith and works in the Jerusalem church was perceived as a threat to their apostolic mission, as an obstacle that had to be overcome for the sake of the gospel and its mission to Jews and Gentiles.

Why is unity so important, even essential? The answer lies in Jesus' prayer, "that all may be one, that the world might believe" (John 17: 21). Unity is not only an end in itself; it is also a means to the end, the end being the mission of the church to evangelize all the nations. The ecumenical movement and the missionary movement are siblings. The problem today is that some churches are internally so confused that they cannot govern themselves in line with their own confessional mandates, inscribed in their own constitutions. The words are fine, but the actions go off in another direction. Churches are being deluged by the tsunamis crashing in upon their shores from the surrounding secular and neo-pagan gnostic culture. That is true not only of the mainline Protestant denominations, but also of the Evangelical and Catholic Churches. It may surprise some to include the Catholic Church in this indictment. But here is what Avery Dulles wrote, and he was an astute observer of the contemporary Catholic scene: "Especially perhaps within Roman Catholicism, a doctrinal crisis is going on."[75] When the rules conflict with surging cultural trends, some church leaders call for a change of rules. This is what happened when the ELCA adopted the "Social Statement on Human Sexuality" (2009) that recommends the ordination of gay and lesbian clergy involved in homosexual partnerships. The document declines to call such relationships marriage. This means that it condones sexual behavior outside of marriage by homosexual persons but condemns it when carried on by heterosexuals. The rules for the rostering of clergy had to change to accommodate the recent shift in cultural trends. The result has been painfully destructive on the church as a whole and on hundreds of its pastors and congregations.

There is no binding authority in any of the Protestant churches that can quell the storm. The Roman Catholic Church majors in authority. Yet, even such an authoritarian system was no match for the conditions that have led to millions of dollars paid out to victims of sexual abuse by their own church leaders, both bishops and priests. Whole dioceses have had to take on bankruptcy. And what is reported in the press is only the tip of the iceberg. Authorities have compounded the wrongs by trying to cover up the scandals with a cloak of secrecy. To the credit of Pope Benedict XVI, he has spoken and acted courageously to meet the crisis head-on.

What can people do if they do not approve of what is going on in their church? Churches in the United States are voluntary associations. People are free to shop around for a church to their liking. The Gallup Poll indicates that Americans no longer feel a strong loyalty to the particular denomination in

119

which they were raised. It is easy to swap churches. Declining congregations are always happy to welcome new members to increase the number of annual pledges in financial support. Many pastors and lay people, as well as theologians, are leaving denominations deemed to be unfaithful to their confessional standards. Some of my fellow-theologians have left the ELCA for what they believe are greener pastures. They have done what they believe is necessary for themselves and their families. I have not been tempted to follow suit, though I am fully aware of the aberrant tendencies in the mainline Protestant denominations. All the churches are in the same boat; none is without its own internal difficulties.

A theologian recently wrote to me about his predicament. He began the study of theology in a seminary of the Lutheran Church–Missouri Synod. In studying the ancient fathers of the Eastern Church, his convictions drew him to Orthodoxy. He attended St. Vladimir's Theological Seminary in New York and became an Orthodox priest. He received his doctorate in theology, making a special study of the relations between Orthodoxy and Roman Catholicism. His findings convinced him that there is insufficient reason to continue the schism between Rome and Constantinople. So he swam the Tiber, as they say, and became a Roman Catholic, serving as a parish priest and teaching in a diocesan seminary. The term "ecumenical chameleon" came to my mind. To make one switch is difficult for me to ponder, but to make two in a lifetime would be hard to imagine.

This is what this person wrote to me: "My situation in a nutshell is the following: from the inside I have come to understand more fully the Catholic system in its 'renewed' conservative form, and as a result, I am internally dying. The rigidity, authoritarianism, corruption, clericalism, and unwillingness to face the truth of clergy sexual abuse (an issue that has pushed my wife to the wall) are all alive and well and thriving here. And I have had to face the rather disconcerting truth that I am, at a theological and spiritual level, not a Catholic, at least in the Roman sense. I am miserable, I feel like a sham, and I'm lost without a sense of direction as to what to do with the rest of my life and ministry. I am 53 years old. I have always wanted and struggled to be an orthodox catholic Christian (which is what my ecclesiastical pilgrimage has been about), but what I have discovered is that being a Catholic in communion with the Roman Church at this point in history is related, but not identical, to that. And the reality is that I don't know what to do with this. I learned to love catholic Christianity when I was a Lutheran, and so my instinct is somehow to turn to it again for help. I am just reading your book, *Mother Church*, and so much of what you wrote resonates with my experience and my theology. That's the reason I'm writing to you."

I responded that I do not believe that being an ecumenical Christian today means shopping around for the more perfect church. That can lead to the kind of disillusionment this unhappy theologian is experiencing. The church is an asylum of sinners, with no exception. My own self-understanding is that as a Lutheran I can try to be evangelical without being Protestant, catholic without being Roman, and orthodox without being Byzantine. I believe there are persons in all denominations with a similar story to tell, persons not reducible to the stereotypes of any single denomination.

Perfect church unity will never exist before the eschaton. Karl Barth rightly said that is an eschatological hope. As long as there is sin and pride within the Christian body, there will arise heresies and schisms, due to ignorance, arrogance, and lust for power. Just as perfect holiness will not be achieved by any individual here on earth, so also no single church will ever become perfectly holy, without spots and wrinkles, in all its structures and actions. This does not mean that Christians should abandon the pursuit of holiness, nor does it mean that churches should give up on their quest for full visible unity. The marks of the church, its oneness, holiness, catholicity, and apostolicity, are not descriptive of what is already the case, but prescriptive of goals to be pursued to the end.

The *Princeton Proposal* is a call to reclaim the priority of Faith and Order. This does not entail the neglect of "Life and

Work" and commitment to the cause of peace and justice. The Proposal charges that today's conciliar ecumenism — the World Council of Churches and the National Council of Churches USA — has deviated from the fundamental vision projected at the New Delhi Conference in 1961. These official organizations are largely captive to a new ecumenical paradigm that subordinates the concern of the "faith and order" movement that gives priority to the unity of Christians and churches, and instead they pursue social and political agendas that inevitably reflect the divisions of the secular realm.

The *Proposal* will be a disappointment to some people, including myself, in that it did not achieve a significant breakthrough in terms of ecclesiology. The study very soon struck the reefs of disagreement on basic issues of ecclesiology, the very ones we enumerated in our discussion of the Lutheran-Catholic dialogue on the "Church as Koinonia of Salvation." No agreement was reached on the structures of the church and ministerial orders. And none on authority, most of all papal authority.

While the *Princeton Proposal* did not succeed in breaking up the ecumenical logjam on these most divisive issues, that is a predicament it shares with all other ecumenical statements, including the most celebrated ones such as *Baptism, Eucharist, and Ministry* as well as the *Joint Declaration on the Doctrine of Justification*. Members of the Study Group agreed with something Pope Benedict XVI has said on more than one occasion. "The way forward is hidden from us. We must prayerfully await an unforeseeable intervention of the Holy Spirit." That is very true, but that should not be used as a cop-out, to diminish our commitment to the goal of the ecumenical movement, namely, full visible unity of churches and Christians, not knowing in advance the shape of things to come under the guidance of the Holy Spirit.

Walter Cardinal Kasper, former President of the Pontifical Council for Promoting Christian Unity, put it this way, in answer to the question: "How long shall we have to wait?" He said, "I am no prophet. I do not know. But I am convinced that one day the gift of unity will take us by surprise just like an event we witnessed on a day already more than ten years ago now. If you had asked passers-by in West Berlin on the morning of November 9, 1989, 'How much longer do you think the wall will remain standing?', the majority would surely have replied, 'We would be happy if our grandchildren pass through the Brandenburg gate one day.' On the evening of that memorable day the world witnessed something totally unexpected in Berlin. It is my firm conviction that one day too we will rub our eyes in amazement that God's Spirit has broken through the seemingly insurmountable walls that divide us and given us new ways through to each other and to a new full communion."[76]

The *Princeton Proposal* entered the the ecumenical world at a time when it was devolving into a state of stagnation and disillusionment. Words sometimes used to describe its current state are "irrelevant" and "outmoded." Generally in conservative evangelical churches ecumenism has acquired such a bad reputation that the very word is hated. Ecumenism is regarded by some on the right as the work of the devil, a threat to their exclusive claim of being the only true Christianity, all others more or less false. The *Princeton Proposal* met with a rather cool reception. The professional ecumenists took umbrage at the criticisms leveled against conciliar ecumenism, the WCC and the NCC. For the rest, it was mostly seen as beating a dead horse. We simply did not succeed in jump-starting a new conversation about ecumenism. Like the national economy, the churches we represented were generally in a survival mode. Most of us are members of the dying, or at least declining, churches of mainline ecumenical Protestantism. Moreover, demographic trends do not indicate a speedy recovery any time soon.

There are five major blocs of Christians in the world: Catholic, Orthodox, mainline Protestant, Evangelical, and Pentecostal. The most ecumenical churches are diminishing not only in numbers but also in the energy spent on spreading the gospel to the millions and billions of people who do not believe in Christ and belong to his church. The ecumenical churches are no longer missionary-sending churches. The Evangelicals and Pentecostals do not belong to the conciliar ecumenical institutions. Michael Kinnamon reviewed the *Princeton Proposal* and observed that it represents the "old-style ecumenism" in which "Faith and Order" concerns were primary. He was right about that. The *Princeton Proposal* asserts that ecumenism must return to the vision for church unity spelled out in New Delhi in 1961. It must return to its earlier spiritual and theological roots spelled out in Edinburgh in 1910. That brought the energies of the world missionary movement into the ecumenical conversation. Ecumenism and evangelization belong together. Conciliar ecumenism (WCC and NCC) is running out of energy because it has lost the missionary passion clearly in evidence on its day of birth one hundred years ago. The most evangelistic churches, those at the forefront of making new Christians, are the least ecumenical. The most ecumenical churches are the least evangelistic. The Edinburgh legacy is to link them together in an indissoluble unity. The ecumenical movement must return to its generative missionary impetus. We will discuss this further in the next chapter on "evangelization."

In the end we realize that the future of ecumenism lies in the hands of God. We do not know the details of what God has in store for the churches that confess Jesus is Lord and Savior. We do not know what kind of unity the Holy Spirit is forging in the name of Christ. We do know that his gifts do not drop down from the sky and that he is calling us to pray and work for a renewal of the Pentecostal experience of the early church.

Chapter Four
Evangelization

The last word spoken by the risen Jesus to his disciples is the *locus classicus* of the church's enduring evangelistic mission: "Go therefore and make disciples of all nations, baptizing them in the name of the Father and of the Son and of the Holy Spirit, teaching them to observe all that I have commanded you; and lo, I am with you always, to the end of the age" (Matt. 28: 19-20). It is customary to call these words the "Great Commission." Embedded in it is the trinitarian name of God, which the apostolic church used as a baptismal confession. It also offers the appropriate framework for a comprehensive biblical theology of the Christian mission. It starts not with Jesus and the New Testament but with God the Father who established a covenant with his people Israel. The coming of God's kingdom in the person of Jesus marks the second stage. And the third begins with the preaching of the apostles in the power of the Spirit. Accordingly, the biblical history of salvation is tripartite — the Old Testament, the New Testament, and the history of the church. We live in the final period before the end of time.

Biblical Foundations

The church's abiding task is to carry on the apostolic mission. Mission comes from the Latin word "*mittere*," meaning "to send." Apostolic comes from the Greek word "*apostello*," meaning "to send forth." The apostolic mission is all about sending, someone sending someone else on a journey of service. Jesus sent the apostles into the world to preach the gospel. But, Jesus said, the real origin of the apostolic mission is with the Father. "As the Father has sent me, even so I send you" (Jn. 20:21). Already in the Old Testament there were advance signs of this pattern of "sending and going." God sent Abraham on a journey to a foreign country and he went; God sent Joseph into Egypt and he went. He sent Moses on a mission to liberate Israel from Pharoah. And God sent one prophet after another to preach judgment and liberation to his people Israel. Finally, at the right time "God sent forth his Son" (Gal. 4:4). And, on the day of Pentecost, the Son sent forth the Spirit. And the rest is history — church history.

God's purpose in setting Israel apart from other nations was to prepare the way for spreading the word of his coming kingdom in power and glory throughout the world. God's election of the Jewish people was not to lavish favors on them as an end in itself, but rather as a means to bring about a universal relation between God and all peoples. The first principle of Israel's gift to the nations is her radical monotheism. In Deut. 4: 39 we read: "Know therefore this day, and lay it to your heart, that the Lord is God in heaven and on the earth beneath; there is no other." Israel's historic calling was to witness to Jahweh as the one and only Lord of the nations. Her mission was to bring forth "justice to the nations" (Isa. 42:1) and to be a "light to the nations" (Isa. 42:6). Closely linked to this sense of her vocation was her expectation of a coming Messiah who would bring in the kingdom of God. Israel's messianic hope made her a witnessing people. During the time between the two Testaments, the Jews of the diaspora made converts of Gentiles and taught them the Torah. This helps to explain something of Paul's missionary success in the major cities of the Roman Empire. There he found a ready constituency among some Gentile converts for his message of the dying and rising of a Jewish Messiah.

The Gospels indicate that Jesus limited his mission to the "house of Israel." Matthew 15: 24 quotes Jesus saying: "I was sent only to the lost sheep of the house of Israel." What accounts for the transition from Jesus' particular mission to the Jews to Paul's universal mission to the Gentiles? There can be only one answer — the historical occurrence of Jesus' suffering, death, and resurrection. The apostles were authorized by Jesus to be the first Christian evangelists because they were witnesses of his resurrection appearances. He commissioned them to proclaim the good news of salvation to the uttermost parts of the world. As apostolic emissaries of Christ they were the natural leaders of the congregations they founded. They gathered weekly to celebrate the presence of the risen Lord by breaking bread together and sharing the cup of wine. In the context of preaching and worship the early Christians grew in their knowledge of how to identify Jesus of Nazareth. To be sure, Jesus called himself the "Son of Man." In his earthly ministry he was called a prophet. He was derisively hailed as the "king of the Jews." To some he seemed to act in the role of the Messiah. But no Jews expected that their Messiah would one day suffer and die on a cross. It was on account of his resurrection that a host of christological titles of exaltation were applied to Jesus, such as high priest, prophet, king, Lord, Savior, and Son of God. This escalation of titles did not end until Jesus was designated as the Word of God, not only like unto God, but truly God, of one Being with the Father.

The apostles were not asked to undertake the mission of the gospel to all peoples, everywhere, until the end of time under their own power and direction. Easter was followed by Pentecost. The apostolic witness to the risen Christ was empowered by a tremendous outburst of energy and enthusiasm from the Holy Spirit. This was authorized by Christ himself: "But you will receive power when the Holy Spirit has come upon you; and you will be my witnesses in Jerusalem, in all Judea and Samaria, and to the ends of the earth" (Acts 1:8). This marks the beginning of world evangelization. In a nutshell it is based on the commission of Christ to preach the gospel of the triune God, Father, Son, and Holy Spirit, to all the nations, beginning in Palestine and then going to every

127

corner of the world until time runs out. The proclamation of the gospel gave rise to a new kind of community inclusive of Jews and Gentiles, women and men, rich and poor, adults and children, and virtually every other imaginable classification of human beings. This community is the new people of God, the body of Christ, the temple of the Holy Spirit, and the proleptic realization on earth of God's eschatological kingdom.

The Acts of the Apostles

We believe in the apostolic church. The apostles are the foundation stones of the church, with Christ himself its chief cornerstone. When the last apostles died, the laying of the foundation came to an end once for all. The apostles have no successors in a literal sense. There are no new apostles in later church history. To call someone an apostle would be a misnomer. In the future there would be pastors, bishops, deacons, and evangelists to carry on the unfinished mission of the apostles.

After the disciples received the power of the Holy Spirit to be Jesus' witnesses, the Book of Acts records the spread of the gospel from Jerusalem to Rome. St. Luke's Book could just as well be entitled "The Acts of the Holy Spirit." The Pentecostals feel most at home in this Book, because they emphasize the outpouring of the Spirit at Pentecost and the charismatic gifts. For them Pentecost was not a one time event at the beginning of the church. It is an ongoing phenomenon in the life of believers today. It starts with speaking in tongues. But that's not all. They claim to possess the same gifts that the Spirit bestowed on Jesus and the apostles, especially the power to perform miraculous wonders and signs. Turn on the television and you will see them in full display, from making a lame man walk, bringing the dead back to life, restoring sight to the blind, and exorcizing demons — all in all performing the same kinds of miracles reported of Jesus and the apostles in the Gospels.

There has been a longstanding theological argument in the church history about the charismatic gifts of Pentecost — speaking in tongues (*glossalalia*), healing miracles, and prophecy.

128

The argument is between cessationists and continuationists. Cessationists maintain that the special charismatic gifts ended with the death of the last apostles. The gifts were given by the Spirit of God as a launching pad for the founding of the church. Then they ceased to happen, there being no longer any need for them. This cessationist view was held by most of the church fathers (e.g., Chrysostom and Augustine), and the reformers (e.g., Luther and Calvin), as well as by later theologians (e.g., Jonathan Edwards and Benjamin Warfield).

Continuationists believe the opposite. They believe the charismatic gifts are perennial, still available today to those on whom the Spirit bestows them. They have never ceased. In the second century Montanism, followers of the heretic Montanus, was a schismatic movement that continued to practice the charismatic gifts. Tertullian joined this group, and for this reason was never elevated to sainthood.

What is the argument all about between cessationists and continuationists? What difference does it make? Cessationists maintain that continuing the gift of prophecy, for example, would endanger the principle of the sufficiency of Scripture. It would mean the Spirit of God grants new revelations to inspired persons in subsequent church history, leading to novel teachings and risking a departure from orthodox doctrine. The leaders of the numerous cults and sects in America — as many as the 57 varieties of Heinz food products — believe that they received a direct communication from God that changed the Creeds of traditional Christianity. Joseph Smith, the founder of the Church of Jesus Christ of the Latter Day Saints, claimed to have received a new revelation. The Book of Mormon supersedes the New Testament.

Traditionally Lutherans have been cessationists, following the *Book of Concord*. In general Lutheran pastors do not practice the charismatic gifts of Pentecost, although a few admit to speaking in tongues. Lutheran pastors pray for the sick, but not without also referring them to medical doctors. Only in one case have I heard of a Lutheran pastor claiming to have brought a dead person back to life. As a rule they expect morticians to take care of the dead. While some Lutheran pastors engage in demon exorcism, most will call for psychiatrists to deal with the possessed. How about prophesying about the approaching end of the world? There have been a few Lutheran pastors who hold a millennialist eschatology, like the evangelical Bible preacher, Harold Camping. He posted his prophecy on billboards and park benches: "Judgment Day, May 21, 2011." The day came and nothing happened, a huge disappointment for Preacher Camping. One pundit tweeted this message to the preacher: "Don't feel so bad. After all, it's not the end of the world!" Camping was last reported to have returned to the Bible to revise his prophecy about the end of the world. But he forgot to read the whole story, for the Bible says: "But about that day and hour no one knows, neither the angels of heaven nor the Son, but only the Father.... Keep awake therefore, for you do not know on what day your Lord is coming.... For the Son of Man is coming at an unexpected hour" (Matt. 24: 36, 42, 44).

The message the apostles preached in the churches of Asia Minor was not complicated. They had a firm sense of Jesus' identity. He is the Messiah of Israel, the Lord of the church, and the Savior of the world. Furthermore, he is the object of their worship. This means that as good Jews, fiercely monotheistic, Jesus had to be God, for only God was worthy of worship. Jews had a greater fear of idolatry than death itself. The key to understanding the message the apostles preached was the resurrection of Jesus. The pharisees believed in the resurrection of the dead, but did they believe it happened to Jesus? Paul was a pharisee, and he came to believe in Jesus as God's Messiah, because he met the risen Jesus on his way to Damascus. The Sadducees did not believe in the resurrection, so they turned deaf ears to the apostles' announcement that Jesus had been raised from the dead.

The resurrection of Jesus is an historical event with far-reaching theological significance. For the apostles and the first Christians the resurrection of Jesus is the answer to the question which God in a world that boasts of many gods is the real God.

If we were to ask Peter or Paul, which God do you believe in? their answer would be: We believe in the living God, the God of Israel, who raised Jesus from the dead. That is who God is — the One who raised Jesus from the grave. And for them he is the same God who created heaven and earth, who elected Israel, and who sent his only Son into the world to be born of Mary. The resurrection tells us who God is and which God is the true God among all the alleged gods and idols in the universe of religions. Without belief in the resurrection of Jesus, Christianity would morph into a different religion.

The apostles went from city to city in Asia Minor preaching Jesus as Messiah and King. Why did the religious and political authorities get so upset with them, even accusing them of "turning the world upside down" (Acts 17: 6)? The apostles were accused of preaching the treasonous overthrow of Rome. In proclaiming Jesus as King, they were charged with sedition, of stirring the pot of rebellion against the imperial decrees of Caesar. In the eyes of their Jewish and Roman opponents, the apostolic preaching of Jesus as King seemed to pit him against Caesar. If Jesus is King, then he must be a contender for the imperial throne. King Jesus is juxtaposed to the Roman emperor. The added qualification that Jesus' kingdom is "not of this world" was too subtle for those who lacked the context of Jewish apocalyptic eschatology to understand what the apostles meant. The apostles did not intend to position Jesus as a competitor to Caesar. Jesus was not after Caesar's throne. Yet, wherever the apostles went, their preaching stirred things up and often caused a riotous upheaval. That is because what they preached was counter-cultural, a message with a moral imperative that called for an alternative way of life.

The preaching of the apostles had an economic effect. It undercut the traditional pagan practice of sacrifice to the gods. If the "gods made with hands are no gods at all," the sacrifices are rendered empty and pointless. The business of making images of Artemis, the great goddess of Ephesus, dried up. The apostles were shaking the foundations of the pagan culture of the Mediterranean world. And for that they were stoned, beaten with rods, stuck in prison, put on trial, harassed, mocked, and driven out. All they were doing was preaching in a way that threatened the practices of sacrificing to the gods, soothsaying, magic, and emperor worship.

One cannot help but wonder why the preaching going on in the churches today, let us say in Europe and America, fails to cause much of a stir. Nobody gets hurt, and there's no price to pay. Is this because everything is all right with the world? Is there no contradiction between Christianity and contemporary western culture, no fundamental difference between a Christian lifestyle and the socially accepted moral practices of the majority around us? Or is it possibly the case that Christianity — Catholic, Evangelical, and Mainline Protestant — has become so thoroughly co-opted by the contemporary neo-pagan culture of death and decadence, that it has lost its transcendence, its potential for conflict, its chief points of metaphysical and moral difference?

Theology of Mission and the Mission of Theology

Most of the first evangelists and missionaries were martyred for their witness. Very few died of old age. But one thing is sure — none of them became theologians or professors. Theology as disciplined reflection on the biblical faith and the church's mission began first with the apologists in the second century — Justin Martyr, Tatian, Athenagoras, and Theophilus of Antioch. Theology did not begin as a luxury for eggheads, for intellectuals who liked to think and write books. Theology became a necessity when Christianity encountered severe opposition on three fronts — Judaism, Gnosticism, and Pagan philosophy and religion. Christians were attacked by Jews as heretics because of their belief in Jesus as Messiah; to the Gnostics Christians were seen as kind of stupid, lacking real knowledge of the deep mysteries of God, and the Roman authorities treated Christians as aliens, adherents of an illegal religion. The apologists came to the defense of Christianity, proving that its beliefs were true and that it posed no threat to the Empire.

Martin Kähler wrote around a hundred years ago: "Mission is the mother of Christian theology."[77] Theology is an essential accompaniment of a missionary church where it encounters threats and opportunities along the way. Academic theology becomes boring when it is not engaged with what Christians are thinking and what the church is doing for God and the gospel in the real world. The task of theology is first to inquire into the nature of the gospel, its biblical foundations, doctrinal contents, and ethical implications, and second to search for the relevant cultural points of contact to guide the leadership of the church in the ever-changing missionary situation. Where there is no gospel, there is no mission. Where there is no mission, there is no church. And where the church is not on a gospel mission, there can be no harvest of faith and discipleship. When churches are dying, it is usually not from external persecutions, at least not in the United States; it is rather from heart failure, loss of faith, and lack of passion for the gospel and its mission.

When theologians are doing their job, they are critical of the church bureaucracy and hierarchy, among other things, whenever these are distracted from the church's primary mission of evangelization. It is understandable that theologians are loved the most when they sidle up to church officials and become members of a society of mutual admiration. But it is hard for theologians to do that when they happen to stand in a tradition that takes its cues from a Luther who wrote the "95 Theses" or from a Kierkegaard who wrote *Attack Upon Christendom*. Luther and Kierkegaard loved the church, but they loved the Lord of the church even more. The church always stands in need of being reformed (*ecclesia semper reformanda*) in light of the critical Word of the law and the gospel.

I have had to answer the question more than once, "Why do you always criticize the church?" Some years ago (1991) I was asked to be the coordinator of a theological conference to address problems of the church and its ministry in the ELCA. The conference was sponsored by three journals, *dialog*, *Lutheran Forum*, and *Lutheran Quarterly*. The title of the

133

conference was "Call to Faithfulness." It aimed to provide a critique of the novel directions the church's leadership was taking the ELCA. The editors of the three journals who spoke at the conference minced no words. Their criticisms were heard around the church. The response from church headquarters was at first to boycott the event and then to ignore the criticisms. In an effort to engage the church leadership in a theological conference that addresses issues of ministry and mission, we invited the presiding bishop of the ELCA to speak at the second "Call to Faithfulness" conference. The theme of his address was "Love this Church." The implication was that those who criticize the church are lacking in love. Nothing could be further from the truth.

But criticism is not the chief task of theology. The accusatory voice of criticism within the church is sounded for the sake of its mission, so that its propagation of the gospel to the glory of Christ does not succumb to the temptation of self-serving propaganda. To do this it will defend the absolute truth of the gospel in face of the current isms that deny it (atheism, secularism, scientism, materialism, gnosticism, mysticism, neopaganism) and it will engage in the perennial hermeneutical task to so shape the interpretation of the gospel that its message might be heard and heeded today.

Every good preacher knows that it makes no sense to take every single word and sentence in the Bible literally. Therefore biblical texts must be interpreted by obeying the hermeneutical principle — interpret the parts in light of the whole. Somehow what the Bible says must mesh gears with what the world needs to hear now. That is the task of theology, to help to make the two ends meet, the Bible, on the one hand, which was written a long time ago in languages foreign to us, and the present world situation, on the other hand, which is a rapidly changing mission field, due to the impact of globalization, the digital revolution, and the growing imbalance between the poor and the rich. It is difficult to be less than apocalyptic about futurological extrapolations of the accelerating pace of famine, disease, violence, ecological crises, nuclear disasters, over-population, poverty, and the list goes on. This is the world we live in and theology must accept its responsibility to think with and for the church to be ready in mission for every eventuality.

Theology today needs to tighten its links to the mission of the church to regain its integrity and credibility. The mission of theology is to be a theology of mission. Otherwise it tends to degenerate into a system of abstract ideas with no relevance to what is going on in the real world. If we were to name theologies of this kind, the list would be long. But even our confessional theology from the age of Luther and the Reformation did not envision a gospel extending to the far corners of the world beyond Christendom. Luther wrote, "No one has any longer such a universal apostolic command, but each bishop or pastor has his appointed diocese or parish."[78] Reasons, or better excuses, have been dreamed up to explain the non-missionary origins of Lutheranism, and of Protestantism in general. Luther had his hands full in reforming the church and opposing the papacy; his followers were busy establishing the Lutheran confession in territories ruled by princes sympathetic to the Reformation, and so forth. But the fact is that the Confessions do not project a vision of world evangelization. The great Lutheran dogmatician, Johann Gerhard, even put forward the incredible notion that the Great Commission of Jesus was fully accomplished in the age of the apostles. After that the church supposedly had only to preach the gospel and administer the sacraments where Christianity was already established as the official religion of the empire.

That kind of thinking changed with the emergence of Pietism, which had its own axe to grind with Orthodoxy. Pietists coined the phrase "dead orthodoxy." It was a cheap shot, because Orthodoxy was very much alive to the intellectual challenge of creating a distinctive system of evangelical theology over against the various forms of Protestantism to the left and their Roman Catholic critics to the right. The fact is that Pietism did not set out to change the doctrinal system of Orthodoxy. But it had an ear for the new voices that called for sending missionaries to preach the gospel to foreign lands. Pietists such as Philip Spener, August Hermann Francke, and

Count von Zinzendorf were convinced that a living faith meant to share the love of Christ with those who have never heard the gospel. In time the divorce between theology and mission that prevailed in Orthodoxy was overcome in the wake of the prolific missionary activity of the Pietists.

The theology of mission in Pietism tended to be individualistic and otherworldly. The missionary Pietists were imbued with a burning zeal to save souls and to plant churches in foreign lands. That was their strong point, and today the growing churches throughout Africa are the beneficiaries of the self-sacrificing service of thousands of missionaries from Germany, Scandinavia, the British Isles, and the United States. Theologically they retained the basic beliefs of Orthodoxy, only their emphasis was different. They were doers of the Word, and less given to parsing the finer points of doctrine. Today African churches are known for their resolute adherence to the biblical, doctrinal, and spiritual substance they learned from their missionary teachers, while their overseas mother churches — Anglican, Lutheran, and Reformed — have increasingly drifted into liberal theology whose priorities stem from the Enlightenment rather than from either Orthodoxy or Pietism.

The Enlightenment brought into play the categories of reason and experience, counterbalancing Scripture and church tradition as the primal sources of theology. Two things happened: first, the rise of historical criticism in the study of the Bible had the effect of relativizing its authority, and second, the rise of the empirical study of the world religions had the effect of treating Christianity as merely an equal of all other religions. Two catchwords sum up the paradigm shift brought about by the Enlightenment: relativism and pluralism. The Orthodox and Pietist theologians put up a strong defense of traditional Christian beliefs, but they could not stop the spreading influence of the Enlightenment on the theology and mission of European and American denominations. Today, all the mainline churches are reaping the whirlwind of the Enlightenment's thoroughgoing transmutation of the classical formulations of Christian theology.

While that is true, a balanced assessment of the Enlightenment will need to take into account the positive achievements of the Enlightenment that virtually no one today would wish to negate. In the providence of God the leading thinkers of the Enlightenment pleaded for religious tolerance, the right of individuals to choose their own religion and to express their convictions freely without political or ecclesiastical interdiction. Coercion is no longer a legitimate method of evangelism. A new attitude of Christians toward persons of other religious persuasions is a plus. Today most religious communities strive for non-authoritarian styles of governance. The disestablishment of religion from state control is prized as a good thing and the idea of separation of church and state is no mere slogan. These are values we all cherish, thanks to the new ground that was broken by the free-thinkers of the Enlightenment.

Yet, the cumulative impact of the Enlightenment on the Christian understanding of the mission of the gospel in the world has been devastating. With the loss of any transcendent eschatological point of reference, the idea of salvation devolved to little more than emancipation from religious superstition, concern for human welfare here and now, and the moral education of the human race. Christianity was viewed as one expression of an underlying universal essence common to all the religions; its significance lay more in the rational morality it teaches than the biblical faith it preaches. Accordingly, the aim of the Christian mission is merely to help other religions become more enlightened agents of human culture, rather than to convince them of the truth of biblical revelation or to convert them to Christ and the gospel. It is easy to see how such an ideology has played out in most of the high level dialogues between Christianity and other religions sponsored by the World Council of Churches.

Mission and the Kingdom of God

Ernst Troeltsch wrote at the end of the nineteenth century: "The bureau of eschatology is mostly closed nowadays."[79]

137

Albert Schweitzer gets the credit for re-opening it at the beginning of the twentieth century. He showed that eschatology lies at the heart of the ministry of Jesus and the message of the apostles. This rediscovery of the importance of eschatology in New Testament Christianity gave a boost to rethinking mission theology.

The kingdom of God that Jesus announced, so central in the Gospels, must be understood against the backdrop of Jewish apocalyptic eschatology that flourished at the time Jesus was born. A lot of ink has been spilled by scholars trying to explain eschatology with reference to a series of false either/ors. It refers either to the *present* or to the *future* mode of time; it has to do with *earthly life* here and now or with *heavenly life* hereafter; its focus is on *individuals* and their inner life or on *society* and its progressive transformation; the coming of the kingdom is entirely the *work of God* or it involves *human cooperation*. Those are unacceptable alternatives.

The good news of the kingdom of God is that it is coming "on earth as it is in heaven." The kingdom has *already* come in the person of Jesus, in his message and miracles, and in his death and resurrection. But the kingdom has *not yet* come in the fullness of its power and glory throughout the world of nature and history.

It might seem odd, perhaps even unacceptable, for a Lutheran theologian to anchor a theology of the Christian mission in Jesus and his idea of the kingdom of God. Lutheran theology usually has taken as its central datum and point of departure Paul's teaching of justification by faith. This again is a false either/or. What is unacceptable is any tendency to place Paul's theology of justification over against Jesus' preaching of the kingdom. Paul could not have imagined that he was substituting his theology of justification for Jesus' message of the kingdom. Instead, Paul understood the justification of the sinner as the reception of the vicarious righteousness of God which is a predicate of God's kingly rule (*basileia*). A person cannot enter the kingdom of God except by being clothed in the robes of a righteousness from above. Justification is the answer to the question of how sinners can gain entrance to the kingdom of God. To seek the kingdom of God and to seek the righteousness which God demands are one and the same thing. They come as a gift from beyond the seeker, not as a result of any personal merits or worthiness. Whoever is justified is one of the elect — called, converted, and introduced by the Spirit into the heavenly kingdom of God.

The kingdom of God was the favorite biblical symbol for the mission theology of the Social Gospel. Walter Rauschenbusch's book, *A Theology For The Social Gospel*, gave it classic expression. A generation later Reinhold Niebuhr was very critical of the Social Gospel, accusing it of a shallow concept of sin and utopian in its social expectations. He was right about that. The failure of the Social Gospel theology was its lack of an eschatological concept of the kingdom of God. A purely ethical concept of the kingdom of God that characterized liberal Protestant theology from Albrecht Ritschl to Walter Rauschenbusch and William Hocking banked on an inner-worldly development of history progressively marching toward a better world through moral striving, social reform, and political action.

The lesson to be remembered is that minus eschatology the gospel gets reduced to ethics. Christianity entered the world of history with an eschatological faith. That was the engine that drove its mission forward and outward. But what kind of eschatology? That is a question we will aim to answer in the final chapter of this book. Here we have only put forward the thesis that the gospel of the kingdom of God — eschatologically considered — is the most adequate starting point for a theology of the Christian mission.

The Future of the Christian Mission

The evangelistic mission of the church arises from the universal vision of its eschatological faith. But the missionary enterprise of the churches in Europe and America seems too enfeebled to carry it out. There may be many reasons to account for this, but two are most obvious. Since the missionary outreach of Western Christianity went arm in arm with colonial imperialism, they both suffered the same fate. The missionary with his cork hat didn't look all that different from the colonial official. After World War II the younger churches in Africa called for a "moratorium on missionaries," and the foreign mission offices were willing to comply. Missionaries were told to go home. Furthermore, theology weighed in with its pluralistic theory of religions. What is the missionary imperative if all religions offer somewhat different but equally valid ways of salvation? At the root of the crisis in world missions was not merely that old strategies were not working but it was rather massive confusion about the Christian message. Why is it really necessary to proclaim the gospel of the kingdom of God to the ends of the earth until the end of time? While there is doubt about that, the churches can redefine the meaning of mission and turn their attention to other more tangible needs — feed the hungry, clothe the naked, lobby for justice, pray for peace, and produce social statements that upset their members and that the rest of the world ignores.

Many of the young indigenous churches in Africa and Asia planted by missionaries are flourishing, much more so than their mother churches in Europe and America. The global future of the Christian mission is shifting into their hands. They have the missionary DNA in their blood. At the same time they are facing the same problem that Christianity experienced after it left its home base in Jerusalem and expanded westward into the Graeco-Roman world: how to retain the purity of the gospel without mixing it with religious and cultural elements that betray its very truth and meaning. When the wine of biblical Christianity was poured into the wineskins of Hellenistic spirituality, it produced gnosticism.

Gnostic Christianity rejected the Old Testament and its revelation of the God who created the world, made a covenant with the Jews, and gave Moses the Ten Commandments. Ever since then the twin heresies of anti-Semitism and antinomianism have reappeared from time to time under new names to corrupt the Christian faith. The Gnostic spirit permeated the anti-Judaism of the German Christians during the Hitler era and is now prevalent in the culture-accommodating trends of liberal Protestantism in Europe and America. Syncretism is the name of the mission strategy of seeking relevance by combining biblical Christianity with beliefs and practices of other religions. Amalgamating Christ with paganism has produced the phenomenon known as Christo-paganism. This tends to happen when zealous preaching to make new converts is not accompanied by the painstaking discipline of catecheses. In the early church the *kerygma* was always followed by *didache*. Reaching a person's heart by preaching needs to be reinforced by getting new ideas into his or her head by teaching. Paul called it "solid food" (I Cor. 3: 2).

Global mission in the future will no longer be a one-way movement from the North to the South and from the West to the East. It will be a two-way street, with missionaries from Asia and Africa coming from their young churches to an increasingly secularized and spiritually desiccated West. South Korea now sends more foreign missionaries than any other country in the world except the United States. Mission experts are calling for the re-evangelization of the new pagan masses in Europe and North America. There is a much higher percentage of church-going Christians in Africa than in Scandinavia.

Global mission in the future will become increasingly more ecumenical as traditional denominational loyalties continue to fade away. The spectacular growth of Christianity in China is a case in point. The best estimate is that there are now more than 60 million Christians in China, and virtually none of them call themselves Anglican or Lutheran or Methodist. Two kinds of Christian churches are recognized by the government and the people, Catholics (independent of Rome) and Protestants (without denominational labels).

The future of the Christian mission will need a theology for a pluralistic age that takes seriously the dialogues with people of other religions, without permitting dialogue to be a substi-

141

tute for evangelism. Dialogue is important under the First Article of the Creed, that is, to promote greater mutual understanding, tolerance, and peace among people regardless of their religious persuasion. The aim of dialogue is not to produce a syncretism of bits and pieces from each of the religions. That only blurs the distinction between faith in Christ and other religious loyalties.

The betrayal of the uniqueness and finality of Jesus Christ in the dialogue of the religions is apostate. Some theologians in every denomination, including among Catholics, are calling for a new approach that no longer aims to convert persons to Christ and to plant new churches. Dialogue works best, they say, when we abandon the biblical-Christian belief in the universal need of salvation through Christ. Christ is interpreted as a symbol of what God is doing in all the religions. All religions are supposedly on a par and equally valid as ways of salvation. The idea of ecumenism should be broadened, they say, to embrace not only Christian churches but all the world's religions. In this wider ecumenism no one is expected to convert from one religion to another. The aim of the Christian mission is simply to engage in dialogue for the sake of a cross-fertilization of ideas. We should be clear, the advocates of a pluralistic theory of the religions — Protestant liberals like John Hick[80] and Catholic modernists like Paul Knitter[81] — are trumpeting a different gospel, not the apostolic gospel of New Testament Christianity.

A major issue in global mission is how women and men relate to each other, not only in the general society but in the context of the church. This continues to be a touchy subject, because some of our partner churches, both at home and abroad, still treat women as second class citizens. Catholics, Orthodox, Southern Baptists, and some Lutherans believe that women by the design of God the Creator should be content with their traditional roles in patriarchal societies defined by the three Cs: Children, Cooking, and Church. In German it is the three Ks: *Kinder, Kuchen, und Kirche.* Not only do they quote the Bible but some argue from natural law. One

142

does not have to be a friend of radical theological feminism to support the rights of women for equality and basic fairness. My view is that the opposition to the ordination of women, from the pope on down, is due to cultural lag, and that it doesn't have a biblical leg to stand on. If that is heresy, I plead guilty. Especially in traditional cultures as in Africa and Asia where women still suffer discrimination, it is important for churches to exhibit a truly egalitarian model of how women and men can relate to each other, honor, and respect each other.

Anyone who knows anything about economic issues is aware that a growing proportion of women and households headed by women are living in desperate poverty. Sober analysis indicates that this situation is caused by the perpetual disadvantage of women in the labor market, their lack of access to education, resources, credit, landownership, inheritance and minimal participation in decision-making. These seemingly mundane matters have a lot to do with the future success of the church in global mission. The gospel must not enter a society and leave things the way they are. These concerns are particularly urgent in developing societies where often women are treated like chattel.

Mission in the third millennium will need to function differently in a shrinking global village. When my parents went as missionaries to Madagascar, it took six weeks to go by sea on a small freighter. Now we can fly there in a day. A letter would take two months to reach the United States. Now we live in an age of mass communications. The computer, faxes, e-mail, satellite hookups, and the internet are having an enormous impact on the life of every man, woman, and child. Religion is affected by these revolutionary changes. Churches that learn how to use the media technologies and the world of cyberspace will be way ahead of the game.

The Christian mission is about more than saving souls for everlasting life with God in heaven. It is that, but it is more than that. The gospel is for life in all its dimensions, not merely the inner life and the afterlife. The concept of holistic mission includes care for the earth. The ecological threat calls the church to the frontline of stewardship for the whole of God's creation, for a sustainable future of life on an endangered planet. As stewards of God's creation, such issues as global warming, over-consumption, and gene technology pose new challenges.

Realists forecast that human suffering will greatly increase in this millennium, due to poverty, over-population, disease, famine, natural disasters like tsunamis and earthquakes, as well as ethnic and religious conflicts. How will Christians witness to Christ as they live amidst the realities of a world torn by domestic and international violence, living in the shadows of nuclear annihilation, poverty in the face of plenty, high mortality and morbidity rates alongside advanced scientific and medical knowledge? All these things the churches will need to ponder as they become engaged in diaconal works of mercy in a suffering world. What does it mean to lay down our lives for others, to show forth the kind of love by which we have first been loved? None of these challenges can be met unless the churches realize the potential of ecumenical cooperation on a worldwide scale. No single denomination by itself can make much of a dent. Because of its greater numbers and resources the Roman Catholic Church is in the best position to take the lead, and most if not all other churches will be happy to be involved.

Edinburgh 2010

Two ecumenically representative missionary conferences were held in 2010, each one planned to celebrate the centenary of the World Mission Conference of 1910 in Edinburgh, Scotland. One was held in Edinburgh, June 2-6, 2010, and the other in Cape Town, October 16-25, 2010. Although the 1910 conference in Edinburgh was on world missions, it is widely regarded as the motivation of the modern ecumenical movement. 1200 delegates gathered, almost all white European and American from the mainline Protestant churches — no Catholics, Orthodox, or Evangelicals. Modern Pentecostalism was just coming into existence at about this same time in Azusa, California. John R. Mott, an American Methodist layman greatly influenced by Dwight L. Moody, was the inspirational leader of the conference. The motto of the conference was "the evangelization of the world in this generation." But based on their experiences in the field, veteran missionaries were convinced that such a vision would be impeded if churches and mission societies remain divided and compete rather than cooperate with each other. Their message of the love of Christ was belied by their loveless behavior. The call for church unity was for the sake of world mission.

Edinburgh 2010 was a very different kind of conference. 290 delegates attended, and only for four days. It was fairly representative of the entire ecumenical spectrum, from Catholics and Orthodox on the right, Evangelicals, Pentecostals, and Independents on the left, and Protestants from the mainline denominations that stem from the Reformation in the middle. They spent a lot of time praying and worshipping together, but for all their talk about the need for unity they could not gather at the Table of the Lord. This was felt by many to be a fundamental contradiction.

In preparation for the conference nine commissions produced study documents that dealt with the paramount challenges facing churches engaged in world mission today. They were: 1) Foundations for Mission; 2) Christian Mission Among Other Faiths; 3) Mission and Post-Modernities; 4) Mission and Power; 5) Forms of Missionary Engagement; 6) Theological Education and Formation; 7) Christian Communities in Contemporary Contexts; 8) Mission and Unity; 9) Mission Spirituality for the Kingdom of God. These nine key themes were carefully chosen to articulate in a comprehensive way the belief of the organizers that a new paradigm is needed for the global mission of Christianity in the twenty-first century.

From my perspective the 2010 Edinburgh conference on world mission failed to lay out a new paradigm. It devoted volumes to sociological analysis but tiptoed around the profound theological issues. It talked a lot about the mission but not about the message. Voices from around the world were heard as they described the challenges and opportunities in their regions, but they too skirted gospel issues that might appear controversial. The conference concluded with a "Common Call" that was supposed to set forth what it means to do missional theology in a new way. Participants from the various streams of the worldwide church joined in a ringing affirmation of this summons to do mission in the new paradigm. However, the "Common Call" is theologically vacuous. It offers no compelling vision based on the Scriptures and the classical creeds of historic Christianity. It mentions the "Triune God," but avoids the proper name of God as "Father, Son, and Holy Spirit." The "Holy Spirit" is the God of choice, mentioned throughout the document in almost every paragraph. The "Spirit" is made to work overtime, given that the "Father" and the "Son" are asked for nothing and given nothing to do. It does not measure up to the trinitarian theology of the Apostles' or Nicene Creed. "Trinity" and "Triune God" are not biblical names for the God of the Bible. They are shorthand used in a theological essay or lexicon.

The "Common Call" is christologically deficient. It refers once to the "uniqueness of Christ," but that is not a bibilical-Christian confession. Every individual is unique. There is only one of me in the whole world. The uniqueness of Jesus lies in his universal salvific significance, as it says in Acts 4: 12: "There is salvation in no one else, for there is no other name given among mortals by which we must be saved." This manifesto does not reject the pluralistic theory of religion that asserts that all religions are equally valid as ways of salvation. It leaves that question open.

This "Common Call" is also ecclesiologically void. Not even the Nicene confession of the church as "one, holy, catholic, and apostolic" is anywhere affirmed in the document. To engage in a lot of talk about mission without giving attention to the nature and marks of the church as the agent Christ appointed to carry it out is an ecumenical setback, after the huge success enjoyed by the "Faith and Order" statement, *Baptism, Eucharist and Ministry.*

The "Common Call" is equally silent about soteriology, the nature and means of salvation that the gospel proffers. Reference could have been made, for example, to the "Joint Declaration on the Doctrine of Justification," initially an agreement between Lutherans and Catholics, but later accepted also by Methodists. If missionaries and mission societies are unclear about what the Bible says about Jesus as Savior and the salvation the gospel promises in his name, their consensus will hardly provide much energy and direction for the future. The new paradigm for global evangelization will be an empty slogan, because it it was projected without sufficient theological substance.

The preparatory documents fail to identify and counter the false missiologies that account for the collapse of the missionary enterprise in present-day European and American churches and denominations. The pluralistic theology of religion maintains that the aim of the Christian mission is to make Buddhists better Buddhists, Hindus better Hindus, Muslims better Muslims, and so forth. The conference documents are eloquent in critiquing the methods of the nineteenth century missionary movements, their paternalism and association with western colonialism and imperial powers. It is a well-established fact that Christianity is growing in the global south and east and declining in the north and west. The majority of the world's Christians now live in Africa and Asia where two centuries ago there were scarcely any. The heroic Protestant and Catholic missionaries must have done some things right. Once when a missionary was being criticized for the methods he was using, he retorted, "I like my way of doing mission better than your way of not doing it." An Evangelical delegate from Sri Lanka gave a blunt evaluation of the Edinburgh 2010 conference: "I confess I haven't sensed the passion for the Gospel and the deep sense of accountability to God for the nations that resonates through many of the 1910 reports."[82]

Edinburgh 2010 will be valuable chiefly for its multi-dimensional analyses of the world situation in which Christians and churches find themselves today. The preparatory studies and follow-up meetings will no doubt provide useful information for denominational leaders and missionaries vocationally engaged in missions, locally, regionally, and internationally. The seeds of Christian friendship, mutual respect, and inter-denominational cooperation that were planted at Edinburgh 2010 may well bear fruit in the years to come beyond anything we can envision. But its theological emptiness will prevent it from going down in church history as one of the great missionary and ecumenical conferences. A grain of the hermeneutic of suspicion suggests that some guiding hand was at work behind the scenes to make sure that nothing theologically controversial would come before the conference.

Cape Town 2010

The Edinburgh 2010 conference made no theological statements with which radical feminists, liberal Protestants, or religious pluralists would disagree. That is why its statements are bland and mostly irrelevant. The same cannot be said about Cape Town 2010. Cape Town 2010 also understood itself as a celebration of the 100th anniversary of the World Missionary Conference held in Edinburgh in 1910. All in all it demonstrated continuity with the passion for world evangelization of Edinburgh 1910 in a way that Edinburgh 2010 clearly did not. Edinburgh 1910 was focussed on the exclusivity of Christ and his transforming gospel for the world's salvation, notes that were muted at Edinburgh 2010. No doubt many of the delegates at Edinburgh 2010 were confessionally orthodox, but apparently they were not in charge.

Cape Town 2010 was a completely different story. 5000 people gathered for the opening service, opening with the same hymn as the 1910 Edinburgh conference — *Crown Him With Many Crowns*. This was the third Congress of the Lausanne movement, started under the influence of Billy Graham. The first Lausanne Congress was held in Switzerland in 1974; it produced the "Lausanne Covenant." The second Congress was held in Manila in 1989 and produced the "Manila Manifesto." Cape Town 2010 was the third Congress, and it produced "The Cape Town Commitment — A Declaration of Belief and a Call to Action."

Cape Town 2010 was not an ecumenically representative conference. They were all Evangelicals of one kind or another. This accounts for the fact that their statement of belief evinced no signs of intimidation by liberal Protestants, radical feminists, or pluralistic theologians, as evidently was the case at Edinburgh 2010. The "Declaration of Belief" of Cape Town 2010 was trinitarian, naming God as Father, Son, and Holy Spirit throughout the document. It was christocentric, stressing the exclusive role of Jesus Christ in the salvation of the world. It emphasized that the gospel of Jesus Christ was meant for all, including Jews, Muslims, and persons of all other religions and no religion. It specifically repudiated the pluralistic idea that all religions are equally valid ways of salvation.

There was no fundamental difference between Edinburgh 2010 and Cape Town 2010 with respect to their soundings regarding the social, cultural, economic, political, and technological challenges the churches are facing today. The leaders did their homework and described the trends of the times in virtually the same way. Their differences were evident in the way the two conferences articulated their theological response to the rapidly changing world situation — secularization, overpopulation, globalization, urbanization, the digital revolution, the resurgence of non-Christian religions, and so forth.

The delegates coming to Cape Town 2010 left with the same theology they brought to the conference. It was an Evangelical theology, with all its characteristic strengths and weaknesses, typical of the Lausanne tradition. There was no evidence the delegates had benefited from half a century of ecumenical dialogues since Vatican II. They talked a lot about Christ, who alone is "the way, the truth and the life," but said very little about his church. They were clearly focused on verbal witnessing and proclamation of the gospel. They quoted the wonderful slogan of the "Lausanne Covenant" — "the whole church taking the whole gospel to the whole world." But there is no such thing as the whole gospel without the sacraments, baptism and the Lord's Supper. We search in vain for any statements about the traditional "means of grace" that nourish those who become converts to the Christian faith.

Chapter Five
Ethics

T he teaching of Christian ethics must begin where Christianity began. It began with Jesus and his message of the kingdom of God. Lutheran theologians would not be Lutheran if they based their thinking about ethics on Paul or Augustine or Luther or some contemporary theologian. And if Christian ethics begins with Jesus' teachings of the kingdom of God, then eschatology is inevitably brought into play. The reason that ethics is closely linked with eschatology is because Jesus proclaimed the eschatological kingdom of God, a "kingdom not of this world" (John 18: 36). To ignore the eschatological theme would mean to ignore Jesus, because all his words and deeds were framed by his vision of the coming of God's kingdom.

Ethics of the Kingdom of God

In the structure of traditional Christian theology, Catholic and Protestant, eschatology was separated from ethics. Eschatology was treated as the doctrine of "last things," such as the second coming of Christ, the end of the world, the final judgment, the general resurrection, and the like, often interlaced with speculations about the rapture, Armageddon, and the like. Ethics, on the other hand, dealt with moral problems in this life here and now. Helmut Thielicke got it right when he wrote: "Theological ethics is eschatological or it is nothing."[83] Paul Ramsey, a leading American ethicist of the last generation, wrote a text book entitled, *Basic Christian Ethics.* In it he acknowledged that the ethics of Jesus originated in the context of apocalyptic eschatology, but for us modern theologians, he opined, eschatology is basically irrelevant for the way we think about Christian ethics. He wrote, we should remember "that genesis has nothing to do with validity."[84] I would counter this with a statement by T. W. Manson, "We must recall the fact that the ethic of the Bible, from beginning to end is the ethic of the kingdom of God."[85] Amos Wilder demonstrated in his book, *Eschatology and Ethics in the Teaching of Jesus*, that the ethics of Jesus was oriented to eschatology through and through.[86] Wolfhart Pannenberg gave this line of thinking a major impetus in his book, *Theology and the Kingdom of God.*[87] Christian ethics is eschatological ethics, not only because that is where it began with Jesus, but also because Paul's letters are all written within the horizon of early Christian eschatology.

The idea of the kingdom of God fell into disfavor in some circles because it was misinterpreted by the Social Gospel movement to mean that the kingdom would be brought about as a result of human moral action and the progressive development of history. For this reason Jesus' concept of the kingdom of God played no significant role in dialectical and existentialist theologies. These were critical of the utopianism of the liberal theologians, in particular the idea that God is using the good works of human beings, especially enlightened Christians, to bring about the kingdom of God on earth. Critics of the Social Gospel theology, like Reinhold Niebuhr, threw the baby out with the bath. When hearing of Pannenberg's proposal to base ethics on the kingdom of God, Niebuhr is reported to have said, "We have been through this business before."[88] He was referring, of course, to the Social Gospel theology. For Niebuhr the background of Jesus' ethics lay in Old Testament prophetic religion, not in the Jewish apocalyptic eschatology that arose in the period between the Two Testaments.

Pannenberg was not returning to the idea of the kingdom of God that prevailed in the liberal Protestant theology from Albrecht Ritschl to Walter Rauschenbusch. The coming of

God's kingdom is not brought about by human ethical activity. That would only result in building a Tower of Babel. Pannenberg used the idea of prolepsis to explain how God's eschatological kingdom is present in the person and activity of Jesus. Prolepsis is a figure of speech by which a future reality is spoken of as though it were already actually present. In the case of Jesus the future kingdom retains its futurity in the very historical events enacted in his ministry. The parables and miracles of Jesus are "signs of the kingdom." They announce, anticipate, and approximate the future and final destiny of humanity and the world under the reign of God. Just as the eschatological rule of God was proleptically present in the words and deeds of Jesus, so also the power of that same reality can be effectively present and give shape to the ethical acts of Jesus' followers.

The order of things is stated in the *Lord's Prayer*: First, thy kingdom come, then, thy will be done. Ethical acts that do the will of God are signs that prefigure the coming reality of God's kingly rule. The futurity of the kingdom retains a critical distance over against the present, so that every human action and every social form are never perfect, but at best partial embodiments of the future kingdom, giving no one cause for boasting before the Lord who judges all things. At the same time, though never perfect the ethical actions of Christians may be a real participation in the new creation that God promises to bring about, effecting change for the betterment of personal and social life in the present. The eschatological kingdom of God in Christ inspires a vision of hope and courage to act in a world under the swaying powers of sin, death, and the devil.

According to New Testament ethics, love is the definitive content of the reign of God to which Jesus submitted himself in absolute obedience, devotion, and trust. Eschatological ethics is therefore *agape* ethics, but not in a reductionist sense as though love abolishes the rule of God's law in the structures of creation embedded in all of life. Jesus was no antinomian. He said, "Do not think that I have come to abolish the law or the prophets; I have come not to abolish but to fulfill" (Matt. 5: 17).

The unconditional love of God that Jesus expressed in his life and ministry does not annul the validity of the Ten Commandments in the Christian life, as taught by the new morality of situation ethics.[89] In the same passage of Matthew Jesus also said, "For truly I tell you, until heaven and earth pass away, not one letter, not one stroke of a letter, will pass from the law until all is accomplished. Therefore, whoever breaks one of the least of these commandments, and teaches others to do the same, will be called least in the kingdom of heaven; but whoever does them and teaches them will be called great in the kingdom of heaven" (Matt. 5: 18-19). Thus, the law and commandments of God retain their binding character for all people, even for Christians, because the last we checked, "heaven and earth" have not yet passed away. A misguided appeal to agape ethics can lead to antinomianism, a denial of the applicability of the law in the Christian life in the name of Christian liberty. The result is license, counterfeit liberty.

There are other theories of moral obligation and moral value. Two common ones are deontology and teleology. Deontology says: Do your duty and do what is right for its own sake. Teleology says: Strive for the good and do what will achieve a good end. Which of these two is more closely related to an eschatological ethics of *agape*? Both. We ought to love God and our neighbors as ourselves because it is the right thing to do. It's the commandment of God. It is equally true that we ought to love God and our neighbors as ourselves because it is the good thing to do. We have God's promise of blessedness. I see no reason to play one off against the other. In a Christian ethics of love we seek to do the will of God by the power of his love because it is both right (our duty) and good (our delight) so to do. "We love because he first loved us" (I John 4: 19). The eschatological kingdom of God actively present in the life and ministry of Jesus releases the power of love into all who believe in him. Love is the answer to what is right — a moral obligation. Love is also the answer to what is good — a moral value. The final ethical criterion of what is right and what is good is the love of God incarnate in the person of Jesus Christ. The distinction between deontology and teleology is overcome from the perspective of eschatological ethics.

Paul writes in Romans 13: 10, "Love is the fulfilling of the law." The law tells us what is the right and good thing to do, but the attempt to do so without love leads to pure legalism. Similarly, to disregard the law of which love is the fulfillment leads to pure antinomianism. Eschatological ethics thus is an ethics of fulfillment, engaging both law and love, distinguishing but not separating them. It is always right to love; it is always an obligation based on the imperative of God's will spelled out in his commandments. It is our duty to love each other, as God has loved us, whether we like each other or not. Yet, we cannot live up to God's demands. "You, therefore, must be perfect as your heavenly Father is perfect" (Matt. 5: 48). Only a fool will claim to be sinlessly perfect. Yet, it is a divine imperative. We are commanded to be and to do what is impossible under the conditions of our fallibility and sinfulness. Our best attempts to do what is right and what is good will not put us on the road to salvation. "But seek first his kingdom and his righteousness, and all these things shall be yours as well" (Matt. 6: 33). In Christian ethics we are not dealing with the way of salvation.

We will now elaborate some implications of eschatological ethics, the ethics of the kingdom of God. New Testament scholars have debated endlessly the question whether the kingdom of God is future or present and other-worldly or this-worldly. Traditional Protestant dogmatics tended to interpret the kingdom of God (heaven) as future and other-worldly. For the Social Gospel theology the kingdom of God is this-worldly and future, something to be realized by the progressive and cumulative good works of human beings. For the existentialist theology of Rudolf Bultmann the kingdom of God is this-worldly and present in the moment of decision. For the dialectical theologians following the early Barth of his *Romans Commentary*, the eschatological kingdom is other-worldly and present (coming *senkrecht von oben*), with little relevance for ethics. In eschatological ethics, by contrast, the emphasis lies on the present impact of God's oncoming future kingdom in the person of Jesus and his community in the power of the Spirit. Thus, it is not a question of either/or, either future or present, other-worldly or this-worldly, individual or social. The transcendent future kingdom becomes really present under the conditions of this world in a way that transforms individuals as well as societies.

The power of the kingdom of God makes a difference in the present, introducing something new that overlaps with the old. The New Testament speaks of two aeons. The new age that penetrates the old age explains why Christians sense that their moral options are inescapably ambiguous. Luther's description of Christian existence as *simul iustus et peccator* is a reflection of the overlapping of the aeons, the new and the old.

The ethics of love is expressed as the ethics of justice under the conditions of a sinful world that has not yet been transformed into the new world of God's kingdom. Love that seeks the fulfillment of another person must take the form of justice. Justice is implicit in the principle, "love your neighbor as yourself," for the core of justice is care for the other person. Deeds of justice can be motivated either by the spontaneous generosity of love or the overwhelming pressure of law. Justice is too important a matter to force people who need it to depend on the good will of a loving person. Courts and prisons exist to enforce the demands of legal justice, without regard to whether or not officers of the law are loving persons. Luther's picture of the two hands of God is useful, the left hand of God's justice meted out according to the law and the right hand of God's mercy proclaimed by the gospel of Christ.

The love of God that expresses itself through justice and law becomes concrete in the formulation of rules and regulations that guide ethical decisions and moral actions of human beings. The antinomian idea that love is antithetical to principles of morality entered the church by way of ancient Gnosticism, reappeared among some of Luther's followers (e.g., Johan Agricola and Nicolaus von Amsdorf) and today has become the operational ethic of mainline Protestantism. According to situation ethics, rules cannot be formulated in advance of each new situation, for example, with respect to liberty and equality. The notion that there are no rules, but only situations, is an unrealistic view of the human condition outside of paradise. Even in Eden life had to be conducted under a divine command, "you shall not." It must be conceded, however, that situations do arise in which love must trump the law for the sake of a higher justice. The works and ways of love at times will challenge unjust laws and call for new legislation. The three great examples in my lifetime are 1) the resistance to the racial laws of the Nazis that discriminated against Jews, 2) the civil rights struggle for racial equality in the United States by Martin Luther King, and 3) the fight against white supremacy and the institutionalized system of apartheid in South Africa.

My ethics professor at Harvard Divinity School was Paul Lehmann. He wrote a book entitled *Ethics in a Christian Context* in which he developed what he called "*koinonia* ethics." He claimed that its validity was limited to a particular context, namely, the context of those who believe in Jesus Christ and are members of his church. That is the strength of his argument. Its weakness is that it disavows any claim to universal validity. This means that what Christians believe is morally right and good has no general applicability. It applies only to those inside the ghetto of a Christian *koinonia*. Eschatological ethics is not confined to those who live within the Christian compound. The eschatological future of the kingdom is the power that draws all human beings in the direction of what is right and good, whether they know it or not. The revelation of God in Christ is the highest good which all persons long for incognito in their quest for fulfillment.

Whether people are Christian or not, the Creator has endowed them with a moral compass — a conscience — which directs them to negate evil and to seek what is good. This envisioned good is absent in the present but awaits future fulfillment. The highest good which Jesus identified as the kingdom of God in his message can be seen retrospectively to be the magnetic force at work drawing all people forward on a quest for personal fulfillment. Therefore, the eschatological kingdom of God is the fulfillment of the original creation, not its replacement. On account of sin all have fallen away from the goodness of God's original creation, but they have not fallen into a different creation. To think so is the Manicheaen heresy. The God of redemption is the same as the God of creation. Therefore, the kingdom of God is proleptically present in all the moral systems of humankind as the power of their end and destiny. This presence of the kingdom of God in the universal human striving for what is right and good is called the "natural moral law" in the classical Christian tradition. This is why it is possible for missionaries to go to foreign lands, learn their language, and communicate the Christian message in a way that correlates with the moral dilemmas and spiritual aspirations of the natives. Upon hearing the gospel of Jesus Christ, new converts frequently testify something like this: "This is what we were always looking for. Thank God, this has come as an answer to our prayers." In Africa and Asia today, Christianity has found a home; it is no longer a foreign religion.

God's Two Ways of Ruling the World

Many of the first generation of Christians believed that Jesus would return in their lifetime and bring the world to an end. Even today there are some would-be prophets — eschatological sharpshooters — who read the "signs of the times" and predict that Christ is coming soon. It soon dawned on the early Christians that "soon" can be a very long time. They had to start making plans for the long haul of history, living in the world, and not a friendly one at that.

When it became obvious that the first generation of Christians was dying out and the end of the world was being postponed, the question became pressing: How shall they live in the world? We have in our possession a letter written by an anonymous author to a man whose name was Diognetus. This is how he described Christians living in the world: "Christians are not distinguished from the rest of humanity by country, language, or custom. For nowhere do they live in cities of their own, nor do they speak some unusual dialect, nor do they practice an eccentric life-style.... But while they live in both Greek and Roman cities ... they follow the local customs in dress and food and other aspects of life. At the same time they demonstrate remarkable and unusual character as citizens. They live in their own countries, but only as aliens. They participate in everything as citizens, and endure everything as foreigners. Every foreign country is their fatherland, and every fatherland is foreign. They marry like everyone else, and they have children.... They share their food but not their wives. They are 'in the flesh,' but they do not live 'according to the flesh.' They live on earth but their citizenship is in heaven. They obey the established laws; indeed, in their private lives they transcend the laws of the land."[90]

The image of Christians as "resident aliens" nicely captures the idea that Christians are to be "*in* but not *of* the world." But not all Christians have come to the same conclusion regarding the proper mode of being in the world. Fifty five years ago H. Richard Niebuhr wrote a book entitled, *Christ and Culture*,[91] depicting various ways in which Christians have conceived of their responsibility for the earthly city. He created five models of relationship between religion and society, faith and politics, church and state. These models are ideal types and do not conform precisely to positions held by any particular churches or sects in the history of Christianity. Niebuhr's typology may serve as a useful teaching aid, as long as we do not confuse it with the results of critical historiography.

At one extreme are those who set "Christ against culture." This is the sectarian strategy of withdrawing from the evil world into separate communities. The Amish Christians try their best to do that. They create a Christian enclave of their own apart from the wider human community. At the other extreme is the "Christ of culture" model. Christians of this type tend to be culture-conforming. They blur the distinction between the church and the world, between Christian faith and the "spirit of the age," the *Zeitgeist*. The other three models in between represent the typical Catholic, Calvinist, and Lutheran ways of relating their Christian faith to the surrounding culture. Niebuhr calls the Catholic type "Christ above culture." This is best symbolized by the medieval popes who claimed the right to crown the emperor. The popes asserted their absolute supremacy not only within the church, but everything in the world was subject to their authority. A remnant of this idea can be seen in the presumed right of Catholic bishops to tell Catholic politicians how to vote on particular issues in the secular realm, backed by the threat of excommunication. The Calvinist type is called "Christ Transforming Culture." The city of Geneva, Switzerland, in the sixteenth century was a splendid example. The magistrates attempted to govern the city on the basis of Christian beliefs and principles; those who were unwilling to conform were exiled or executed. Poor Servetus was burned at the stake in Geneva for denying the Trinity.

Niebuhr called the Lutheran view "Christ and Culture in Paradox." This is more commonly referred to as the Lutheran doctrine of the two kingdoms. We will try to explain what this means, although my attempt will be no less controversial than that of anyone else. Greater minds than mine have tried to unpack what Luther meant by the two kingdoms (*Zwei Reiche*) — Ernst Troeltsch,[92] Karl Barth,[93] Anders Nygren,[94] Dietrich Bonhoeffer,[95] Gerhard Ebeling,[96] and Heinrich Bornkamm[97] — and no two of them agree with each other. I have gleaned insights from all of them, but none is responsible for my interpretation of the two-kingdoms doctrine.

Luther credited Augustine's concept of the two cities of God, the earthly city and the heavenly city, for his own teaching about the two kingdoms or two realms of God. The heavenly city refers to the Bible's account of salvation that starts with Adam and Eve in the Garden of Eden and ends with the vision of the saints in the heavenly city of Jerusalem. The road from paradise lost to paradise regained runs through the great cities built by the children of Cain — Babel, Babylon, Sodom, and

Nineveh. Finally, Jerusalem became the battleground city on which Christ defeated the "powers and principalities." The "left hand of God" was Luther's image of the way God administers the daily affairs of human life: marriage and family, as well as political, economic, and cultural matters. God is at work in the world throughout the secular world. For Luther God is working *incognito* by means of public agencies to accomplish his will. The instruments God uses in this realm are the laws of the state and the power of the sword.

Then there is also the "right hand of God," which is God's way of working in history to bring about the salvation of humankind. He does this through the election of Israel, the ministry of Jesus, the founding of the church, the means of grace — Word and Sacraments — and the proclamation of the gospel to all the nations and peoples of the world.

Thus, a certain dualism characterizes Luther's thinking: two kingdoms, two hands of God, two ways of God working in the world. Which raises the debatable question: how are the two kingdoms related to each other? What in the world are Christians to do? What should they stand for in the secular realm? For whom should they vote? Luther and Lutherans in general have been criticized for what has been called "caesaropapism." "Caesar" is a symbol of secular authority, as in Jesus' saying, "Render unto Caesar the things that are Caesar's" (Matt. 22: 21). "Caesaropapism" is a system of government in which the head of the state is also the head of the church. When Luther and his Reformation lost the support of the Catholic bishops, the secular princes were accorded supreme authority over affairs of the church. The princes were called "emergency bishops." In the Nordic countries Lutherans founded state churches with a king or a queen at the head. The worst scenario worked itself out in Nazi Germany, when Lutheran pastors, bishops, and professors signed oaths of allegiance to Hitler, the supreme *Führer*. Those who refused were put in jail, hanged or sent to the gas chambers. Martin Niemöller preached a sermon in Berlin whose refrain was "Jesus is our *Führer*," and he was thrown into prison.

Karl Barth blamed Luther's doctrine of the two kingdoms for the terrible debacle of the German Churches under Hitler. After World War II Lutheran theologians rejected Barth's criticism that Luther's idea of the two kingdoms led like a straight line to Hitler. It wasn't Luther but the apostle Paul who wrote, "Let every person be subject to the governing authorities; for there is no authority except from God, and those authorities that exist have been instituted by God. Therefore whoever resists authority resists what God has appointed, and those who resist will incur judgment. For rulers are not a terror to good conduct, but to bad. Do you wish to have no fear of the authority? Then do what is good, and you will receive its approval; for it is God's servant for good. But if you do what is wrong, you should be afraid, for the authority does not bear the sword in vain! It is the servant of God to execute wrath on the wrongdoer. Therefore one must be subject, not only because of wrath but also because of conscience. For the same reason you also pay taxes, for the authorities are God's servants, busy with this very thing. Pay to all what is due them — taxes to whom taxes are due, revenue to whom revenue is due, respect to whom respect is due, honor to whom honor is due" (Rom. 13: 1-7).

That is the scriptural basis for Luther's idea of the "left hand of God." Lutheran apologists for Luther's doctrine of the two kingdoms believe it is fundamentally biblical and right for the church and the gospel. But to do this they have to admit that it has been badly applied and misinterpreted by Lutherans themselves. It is wrong and anachronistic to blame Luther for the atrocities committed by the Nazis. Luther's doctrine needs to be revised, or at least clarified, so that it does not justify subservience to the powers that be, no matter how demonic. It must be conceded that wherever Lutherans have been in the majority, the two kingdoms doctrine has led to a conservative political attitude that supports those in power, and is generally suspicious of and even antagonistic toward protest movements. This has always struck me as strange, considering that Lutheranism itself began as a protest movement, protesting the two super powers at the time, the pope and the emperor. The first Lutherans, after all, were called protestants — protesters.

To complicate the defense of Luther, critics point to his role in putting down the Peasants' Rebellion. Luther wrote a disgraceful pamphlet, "Against the Robbing and Murdering Hordes of Peasants." In the struggle for racial equality in South Africa Lutheran churches supported the apartheid policies of the white supremacists. In Chile the majority of Lutherans supported the policies of General Pinochet who tortured and killed those who protested the policies of his government that fostered economic inequality and social injustice. During the Vietnam era an American Lutheran bishop wrote a pastoral letter advising, "Don't preach anything controversial." Churches are voluntary associations. When people get upset, they withhold their financial support or simply walk away.

In Defense of the Two Kingdoms Doctrine

Despite such a checkered history, I believe it is possible to retrieve something essential in the doctrine of the two kingdoms. But one thing has to happen first, and that is to overcome the idea held by many Lutherans that faith and politics are completely separate and have nothing to do with each other. Christophe Luthardt (1823-1902), a German Lutheran theologian wrote: "The Gospel has absolutely nothing to do with public life but only with eternal life.... It is not the vocation of Jesus Christ or the Gospel to change the orders of secular life or to renew them.... Christianity wants to change a person's heart, not his social situation."[98] Writing during the Hitler period, another German Lutheran theologian wrote, "There is no contradiction between an unconditional allegiance to the gospel, on the one hand, and a similarly unconditional allegiance to the German nation, that is, to the national-socialist state, on the other."[99] The idea that one can be equally loyal to two masters goes against Jesus' statement, "No one can serve two masters" (Matt. 6: 24). Peter's statement also needs to be invoked, "We must obey God rather than any human authority" (Acts 5: 29). The German Christians who supported the Nazis ignored such qualifications of loyalty to the governing authorities.

A famous Lutheran jurist, Rudolf Sohm, wrote that the issues of public life "should remain untouched by the proclamation of the Gospel, completely untouched."[100] There is a word for this — dichotomy.

Considering the role such dichotomizing of the two kingdoms played in the support of the Nazis, we will have to call it a heresy. Reclaiming the doctrine for the church today is an uphill climb, and yet I think it must be done. Dietrich Bonhoeffer's example of resistance to Hitler's government was a chief inspiration for Lutherans to revisit the doctrine and to get rid of the idea that the two kingdoms are totally separate and have nothing to do with each other. For that would mean that when Christians enter the public arena, they must leave their private faith behind. The split between the private and the public is an idea that has no basis in the Bible. If it did, Jesus would not have been crucified by the Roman government. John the Baptist would not have lost his head to King Herod. If faith is so private as to have no public expression, there would have been no Christian martyrs.

A purely private faith that does not engage the controversial issues of the day will keep a person out of trouble with the authorities. Christian faith that expresses itself in the public realm is always poised between patriotism and protest. There may be good times when faith will express itself as patriotism; there may also be bad times when faith will express itself as protest. The brave freedom riders who took a bus trip through the South and were beaten and jailed were expressing their faith in Jesus. They were not political revolutionaries. One of them was James Reeb, a fellow student of mine and graduate of St. Olaf College, who was murdered during the march on Selma, Alabama, by southern white supremacists, 50 years ago. It has been a life-long regret of mine that I was not one of those who marched. We Lutherans should be ashamed that we have more often been at the tail rather than at the head of the civil rights struggle in the United States. The two kingdoms doctrine lies at the base of the hidebound tradition of support for the established authorities and the status quo. Not many Lutherans marched with Martin Luther King. As Lutherans we have too often leaned on Romans 13 like a crutch. "You must obey the governing authorities." In the South the governing authorities were the likes of George Wallace and Bull Connor. It took many acts of civil disobedience by persons motivated by faith to bring about legislation that put an end to the Jim Crow laws of racial segregation.

Lutherans who have been busy revising the doctrine of the two kingdoms remember that the Reformation began as an act of civil disobedience. Luther was asked to recant and he did not. He defied the emperor. He hid away in the Wartburg Castle. He made amply clear that there are times when it is necessary to resist temporal authorities, to break human laws that violate the justice of God. It is necessary to refuse to bear arms in a manifestly unjust war. Luther did not believe in an unconditional allegiance to the State, when the State commits acts against the law of God. There are times when Christians must conscientiously object, even if it means going to prison, paying a fine, or suffering the ridicule of one's peers. Not many Lutherans have had the 20/20 vision to tell the difference between a just and an unjust war, until perhaps after the war is over. To be sure, there is no basis in Lutheran theology that dictates absolute pacifism, that is, refusing to bear arms under any circumstances. The criteria to distinguish a just from an unjust war have been spelled out in theory, but to apply them in practice is another thing. Was the Revolutionary War a just war? Was the war against the Indians a just war? Was the Civil War a just war? Was the Spanish-American war a just war? Was the Korean war a just war? Was the Vietnam war a just war? Was the War against Iraq a just war? With all these wars in which the United States has been engaged, one would think that we would by now be experts in discerning the difference between just and unjust wars. Lutheran churches like most others are completely unprepared to render a moral judgment when their nations go to war. Patriotism or protest? As Lutherans we must give serious thought to why we almost always come down on the side of patriotism.

Lutheran churches all over the world are deeply engaged in the question of their social responsibility. A large share of every synodical or church-wide assembly is devoted to debates on issues that deal with the secular realm, issues of peace and justice and the environment. This is something virtually new in the history of Lutheranism — the idea that the church should meet in solemn assembly and deliberate not only about its intramural affairs, like the pension program and worship practices, but also about politics and economics and family issues, all of which have traditionally been placed in the left hand of God. Many Lutherans get upset about the trend of having their national church assemblies more involved in disputed questions on the left hand of God than on urgent matters having to do with the right hand of God.

To be concerned about the right hand of God means that Christians will focus on matters of faith and evangelism, how to spread the gospel to unreached peoples, at home and abroad, how to plant new congregations, how to educate future pastors and set standards for ordination, and how to educate new converts to become disciplined believers. To be concerned about matters on the left hand of God is important too, because Christians are called to be stewards of God's world, the whole creation. But Christians should put first things first and remember their priorities. They should remember they are "resident aliens." They stand shoulder to shoulder with all people of good will from other religions or humanists who have no religion at all. In the secular realm people debate the issues that bear on the common life, using reason, conscience, and common sense, but most of all an overdose of self-interest. Christians have no monopoly on such faculties. This means that Christians should give priority in their assemblies to those matters of ultimate concern, without neglecting matters of penultimate value.

The root of the two kingdoms doctrine lies in the answer of the early church to this question: what is the community of the end-time to do in the mean-time? Recall that the first Christians believed that the kingdom of God was coming soon to wrap things up, so they would not have to worry about the plumbing, their next meal, or how to send their kids to college. The kingdom has already arrived in Jesus but it has not yet arrived to set all things right in the world. So we live paradoxically in the tension between the "already" and the "not yet." That was on the mind of the one who wrote that letter to Diognetus. How are Christians to live in the world while they wait for the final coming of Christ to judge and consummate the world? We now enjoy an ecumenical consensus, I believe, that the two extremes we mentioned above, "Christ against Culture" and "Christ of Culture," do not provide the best answers. The first extreme, "Christ against Culture," is that of some radicals who say, "Do not get involved in the world. The rapture will soon sweep us up into a cloud of other-worldly bliss." That is the way of the sectarian apocalypticism that inspired the crazy experiment of Jonesville. The other extreme, "Christ of Culture," goes in the opposite direction, not separation from the world but identification with it, amalgamating Christianity with the wisdom of the age and the moral fashions of the day.

The two kingdoms doctrine offers a middle way between the two extremes of *separation* from the world and *identification* with it. It teaches the fine art of drawing the proper distinction between law and gospel, justice and justification, the works of the left hand of God and the right hand of God, and the two ways of God at work in the world. In the kingdom on the left we may join liberation movements of whatever kind we think advances the principles of justice at the present time, knowing full well that human liberation is not the same thing as Christian salvation. Some liberation theologians teach that liberation and salvation are two words for the same thing. They are wrong. No liberation movement can deliver the salvation that only Christ can give through his death on the cross and

167

resurrection from the grave. The best government in the world cannot preach the gospel. The best social system cannot bestow the love of God and his forgiveness that only the gospel can promise. We say that we live in the land of liberty. Democratic freedom is one of the values our nation is willing to fight for, not only for itself but for other nations, as it did in World War II and is now attempting in the Mideast. But this kind of freedom which is our privilege to enjoy must not be equated with the one thing needful — the freedom of the gospel for which Christ has set us free (Gal. 5: 1). This is the freedom the apostle Paul experienced while sitting shackled in the city jail of Philippi.

Preaching and the Politics of the Kingdom

Some years ago there was a theological debate in Germany on the question: "Must a Christian be a socialist?" Helmut Gollwitzer, a socialist himself, answered "Yes." Christians must contend for socialism. By that he did not mean anything like Marxist communism. By socialism Gollwitzer had in mind a political system that seeks economic equality and social justice for all. That entails breaking down the gap between the rich and the poor. Eberhard Jüngel answered "No." Christians are free to be on the side of capitalism. Precisely here the two kingdoms doctrine comes into play. It says that it is wrong to identify Christianity with socialism or capitalism. We have no scriptural basis to pronounce a divine benediction on any particular social or political system. At the same time, world history records an endless number of demonically oppressive systems that must be opposed by people who fear and love God. The twentieth century had more than its share of them: Hitler, Mussolini, Stalin, Mao Tse Tung, Idi Amin, Milosevic, Kim Jong Il, to mention a few of the most notorious dictators. They oppressed their people and murdered their opponents, including millions of Christians.

In the current political climate in the United States, some seem to think that God is on the side of their party preference, whether Democratic or Republican. There are others who think it helps to reach a moral decision by asking, "What would Jesus do?" From the perspective of the Lutheran two kingdoms doctrine we have no such easy formulaic solutions. We can say this much: It is wrong for Christians not to participate as citizens in the messy world of politics (to vote) and economics (to pay taxes). It is wrong to try to keep one's hands clean and not get involved. But is equally wrong to claim that the party one supports is God's party. Critical participation means one is not a flunkie of any party. A Christian will not say, "My country right or wrong" or "Win at all costs." Critical participation is not lapdog politics but watchdog politics. It is the way of the Christian conscience cleansed by the gospel.

Christians are free from bondage to a particular ideology, whether on the side of socialism or on the side of capitalism. If Christians are not to separate themselves from the world, they must choose the strategy of critical participation in every system in which the church finds itself, and maintain a healthy suspicion of every system that does whatever it takes to hold on to the reins of power. A Christian who has mastered the fine art of drawing the proper distinction between the two kingdoms — the two ways of God working in the world, through the law and through the gospel — should be like a swimmer with head out of water and eyes on the shore, being *in* but not *of* the world.

Should we who accept the Lutheran doctrine of the two kingdoms support the First Amendment of the United States Constitution which in effect stipulates a separation of Church and State, or should we work to rescind it, and try to make the United States a Christian nation? What does the Amendment say? It all depends on how it is interpreted. Some interpret it to mean that it allows no expression of religion in the public realm. Religion is a private matter. It belongs in the heart, in the home, in the church, but never in public schools, halls of justice, or political offices. Does the First Amendment prohibit prayer and Bible reading in public schools, or posting the Ten Commandments in a courtroom, or singing a Christmas carol by a public school choir, or the President saying "God bless America" at the end of all his speeches? Should the words "under God" in the pledge of allegiance be retained? Should the public square be denuded of all religious symbols and observances? Should there be chaplains in the United States military, with their salaries paid by tax dollars? Atheists pay taxes too, but are opposed to what chaplains do. Should there be a Christian pastor or priest in the Congress? If so, should a Jewish rabbi or a Muslim imam take their turns on a rotating basis? Is it right or wrong for a Christian majority to impose their sense of morality on a secular pluralistic society? What protection will they then demand when they happen to be in the minority?

When we sing or pray, "God bless America," should we not invoke God's blessing equally on all nations? Do Christians believe that America is God's favorite nation? Is the myth of American exceptionalism any more justifiable than Alfred Rosenberg's myth of Aryan superiority that supported the racial theories of the Nazis? The idea of American exceptionalism supports the dangerous notion that Americans are God's newly chosen people to spread the gospel of democracy and free market capitalism to all other nations, by all means necessary, including military crusades. Just when the churches quit sending missionaries around the world to preach the gospel of Christ, should American Christians now support their nation in sending armies around the world to propagate a "different gospel" (Gal. 1: 6)? The outcry of "missionary, go home" has been replaced by people in other nations chanting, "Yankee, go home!"

Christians in American face a dilemma. If they take the side of those who wish to keep religion in the public square, such religion will necessarily not be true Christianity but some kind of watered down civil religion. Traditionally Lutherans have not supported "religion in general" or civil religious rituals in which the name of the Triune God or Jesus Christ must be excluded from their invocations and benedictions. Thus, when civil religion is practiced on public occasions, such as

170

Fourth of July, Thanksgiving Day, or Memorial Day observances, it will be deistic, unitarian, perhaps Jewish or Muslim, but never really Christian. Is that what we want? Do Christians really want to pray to a God other than the Father of Jesus Christ and intentionally omit praying "in the name of Jesus?"

The choices are starkly grim. One option is to keep the public space completely secular. Get rid of "In God We Trust" and such phrases. That will make the ACLU and atheists like Madeline Murray O'Hare happy. A second option is to join in the practices of civil religion, reciting its solemn rituals and symbols. But if we do that, have we not then violated the First Amendment by consenting to an official establishment of a religion, namely, the American civil religion? A third option is to support the conservative evangelicals who try to re-Christianize the civil religion. That means to fill public ceremonies with Christian language and substance, the result being that our non-Christian neighbors will feel like Jesus and the Trinity are being rammed down their throats.

I cannot muster much enthusiasm for any of those options. Luther's formula "*simul iustus et peccator*" meshes with my own self-understanding as a Christian. We are saints and sinners at the same time. Some critics do not like this formula; they like to think of themselves as more saintly than sinful. I believe that is the kind of self-deception of which even good Christians are capable. With regard to how Christians should behave in the public square, we must realize that there are situations in which we do not have a squeaky clean option. We are confronted by ambiguity wherever we turn. America is an irrepressibly religious nation, and there is no way that even the Supreme Court or the Congress will prevent Americans from expressing their religious sentiments in times of national emergency, like after the attacks on 9/11. We will sing "God Bless America" as though it were our national anthem. On national holidays we will no doubt participate in ceremonies of civil religion, with goose bumps and all. I will justify this as the practice of faith limited to the First Article of the Creed, and reserve the Second and Third Articles to the practice of specifically Christian worship of the Triune God, Father, Son, and Holy Spirit. This suggestion is inescapably ambiguous under the conditions in which we live in the United States of America, a secular democracy with puritan and deistic religious origins but not a Christian nation by any stretch.

After 9/11 a Missouri Synod pastor in New York City, the Rev. David Benke, participated in an inter-religious prayer service. That is *verboten* by the Lutheran Church–Missouri Synod. He was accused of the sin of unionism. Charges were brought against him and he was removed from his office until the case was reviewed and settled. To make matters worse, he had been given permission from the President of the Synod, and so charges were brought against him too. Which side was in the right? My own view is that a pastor must be allowed a great deal of latitude to play it by ear and use sanctified common sense. Every situation is fraught with ambiguity. Let the person who is without sin cast the first stone. We all live in glass houses. We live in a pluralistic society, so as pastors we need to negotiate our way through the maze when there is no perfect choice. If I make a bad choice, it is not unforgivable. Thank God for "*simul iustus et peccator!*"

As a rule Lutheran preachers have kept politics out of the pulpit. This is not necessarily true of other traditions. The Black Church comes most readily to mind. The name of Jesse Jackson is synonymous with mixing preaching and politics. Every Saturday morning in south side Chicago, Rev. Jackson would lead a service and preach at Operation PUSH (People United to Serve Humanity). And who can forget the ranting and raving of the Rev. Dr. Jeremiah A. Wright, President Obama's former pastor at Trinity United Church of Christ in Chicago? But not only black preachers but Catholic priests are often exhorted by their bishops to tell their parishioners how to vote on certain issues.

Perhaps Lutherans need to take a closer look at the problem of politics in the pulpit in light of the two kingdoms doctrine. If a Lutheran minister should preach the whole counsel of God, that will necessarily include the Word of God in its twofold form, both law and gospel. He or she cannot preach only the gospel and omit the law. The gospel without the law is like an answer without a question, a solution without a problem, like taking medicine when one is not sick. The gospel is the medicine that heals those who are sick. In the kingdom on the left hand, God rules through the law. In the kingdom on the right hand, God rules through the gospel. We do not preach the gospel to Enron or General Motors or Microsoft or Halliburton. We do not preach the gospel to our elected officials meeting in Congress. However, as custodians of the Word of God, both law and gospel, we do have the obligation to preach the law of God and call for it to be observed in the secular world of business and government. That is the political use of the law (*usus politicus* or *civilis*, the first use of the law). Preachers are commissioned to preach both law and gospel. When those who have been elected to uphold the just demands of the law act in lawless ways, they need to be called to account. When laws prove to be manifestly unjust, they need to be rescinded. What is the criterion? How do we know when the law of God in the secular realm is not being observed? We possess a critical standpoint in the idea of justice. Justice is the form that love takes in the secular realm of politics and economics. The sum of the law is: you should love your neighbor as yourself. If you truly love your neighbor, you will serve your neighbor's needs. That is what the story of the Good Samaritan tells us. The Good Samaritan did not preach the gospel to the victim robbed and beaten lying by the roadside. He cared for his neighbor's needs. He took him to an inn, paid the bill and went on his way. But it is understandable that preachers will avoid prophetic preaching. They remember what happened to John the Baptist, and Jesus suffered a similar fate, by sticking his message of the kingdom of God into the face of the ruling religious and political authorities.

How do we know when the church, its elected officers, and its parish pastors are crossing the line, and mixing religion and politics? The IRS goes after preachers who cross the line of separation of church and state, using the pulpit for partisan politics. The law forbids 501(c)(3) organizations to "participate in any political campaign on behalf of or in opposition to any candidate for public office." On the other hand, the First Amendment defends the free exercise of religion and equal protection of the law. It's a sticky wicket. Is it crossing the line of separation of church and state if a minister preaches the law and judgment of God in a way that exposes the pretensions of the powerful and those who co-opt Christian values to mean pro-rich, pro-war, and pro-America? How should the words of Jesus be applied without being accused of crossing the line: "Blessed are the peacemakers, for they shall be called the children of God" (Matt. 5: 9)? What is the cash value of preaching good news to the poor and liberation to those who are oppressed? Should not a preacher speak out against policies that serve the interests of private wealth more than the public welfare? Should not a preacher condemn a system that privileges a few with health insurance, rewarding jobs, excellent education, and good housing, while many are mired in misery and poverty? Can we find any biblical justification for a tradition of preaching keen to focus on private sins but failing to mention public evils? At family gatherings people tend to avoid controversial topics, like religion, politics, and sex. Similarly, at church gatherings people tend to check their deepest convictions that have to do with controversial economic, social, and political issues at the door, so that harmony and happy feelings can prevail within the walls of the church.

The two kingdoms doctrine teaches us the difference between what unites us as members of the body of Christ, matters of ultimate concern in the vertical dimension before the God (*coram deo*) of our salvation, on the one hand, and worldly temporal issues on which we must deliberate and at times disagree, matters of penultimate concern, on the horizontal place before each other and the world (*coram mundo*).

If we agree that we should not preach partisan politics in the pulpit, we might also agree that we do not wish to come to church to hear only the consolations of the gospel of God's grace without the condemnations of the law and the judgments of God's wrath. In this chapter we have offered an apologia for a both/and stance, both law and gospel, neither separating nor identifying the two kingdoms of God, living to the hilt in two cities, the heavenly city and the earthly city, both of them spheres in which God is at work, but in different ways. We cannot preach the whole Word of God, which is sharper than a two-edged sword, if we ignore the issues of war and peace, care for the earth and our bodily health, and the wretched conditions in which millions of our fellow human beings live.

The Doctrine of Creation and the Law of God

The doctrine of the two kingdoms makes a clear distinction between creation and law, on the one hand, and gospel and church, on the other. Creation and law are universal; they refer to structures of the common life into which everyone born into society lives. Gospel and church are particular; they refer to realities specific to persons who believe in Christ and enter his community through faith and baptism. The one sphere includes the orders of creation in which all persons participate in some way — government, work, and family life. God speaks his universal laws through the things that he created, and these laws impinge on the faculties of human reason and conscience that can distinguish right from wrong. A person is born into this sphere. The other sphere includes the special history of salvation transmitted through Scripture, culminating in the incarnation of the Son of God and the founding of the one, holy, catholic, and apostolic church. To enter this sphere one must be "born again."

For this reason Christians have a double identity, citizens as they are of two cities. In the secular realm the church and the unchurched live and work side by side with no legal distinctions. The rule of God in the public orders is not primarily in the hands of believers. God has used emperors, kings, presidents, and politicians who more often than not are not Christians. There is no secular realm in which God is dead. There

175

is no empty world into which believers need to introduce the laws of God. The Gentiles know these things and do not need Christians to tell them. They do not need synodical meetings of Christians to pass resolutions on matters about which they have received no special revelation from God. Christians must use their reason and rely on the facts in evidence as much as anyone else.

We do not expect salvation from the realm of creation and the rule of law. In the kingdom on the left hand of God we are called to promote peace, pursue justice, and advocate freedom, but these actions are not on the same plane as the advent of God's kingdom and its righteousness through Christ. The eschatological kingdom of God in the ministry of Jesus does not come about through the politics of this world, which always involves force and violence.

A strong emphasis on God's rule of law through the orders of creation lets the church be the church. The most effective social witness the church can make happens not through social statements but by being the church and doing all that God has called it do do. The task of the church is to preach Christ. If the church does not observe the proper distinction between the two kingdoms, the most pernicious things can happen in both the church and the world. Either the content of the gospel of eternal salvation is reduced to a social message to ameliorate the conditions of life in this world, or it is equated with the loftiest wisdom of philosophy and heroic examples of morality. Then Jesus is placed on a par with Plato, Confucius, or Karl Marx. Then the eternal peace which surpasses human understanding on account of Christ's victory over sin, death, and the power of Satan, is dismissed as pie in the sky, in exchange for the various approximations of peace and prosperity which in good times this world also knows about and experiences. To distinguish heavenly peace from earthly peace, eternal salvation from temporal shalom, divine justification from social justice, spiritual righteousness from civil righteousness is absolutely essential to maintain the integrity of the gospel and the uniqueness of Christ's mission through the church.

The law of God in the orders of creation is called the natural law (*lex naturalis*) or the law of creation (*lex creationis*). The concept of natural law is not original with Christian theology. Its classical formulation was given by the ancient Greek philosophers, especially Aristotle. They argued centuries before the Christian era that the universe is governed by laws inscribed into the nature of things. Humans are endowed with reason which enables them to know what is in accordance with nature. They are also capable of choosing between what is right and wrong. The church fathers adopted the Greek philosophical theory of natural law, identifying it with the law of God written on the hearts of human beings to which their conscience bears witness, as Paul said in Romans 2: 15. Thomas Aquinas continued the natural law theology of the fathers. Natural law is grounded in the eternal mind of God, which human beings can know by their reason and conscience. The law written on human hearts and in the nature of things is the same for everyone everywhere. The positive laws of the state must be judged by the criterion of the higher law of God, the natural moral law.

Christian theological ethics enters the debate on moral issues in the public square with arguments based on natural law. In Western intellectual history the idea of natural law has formed the backbone of social morality, political philosophy, and legal theory. To ignore this tradition Christian ethics would have to sit in a corner somewhere and talk to itself. It would not be able to address issues of common concern to people of all races, classes, cultures, and religions.

Natural law informed the framers of the Constitution of the United States. The United Nations' Declaration of Human Rights is based on a universal belief in natural law, as valid in Africa and Asia as in Europe and America. We all have too much at stake to see the tradition of natural law abandoned to alternative theories such as utilitarianism, positivism, or postmodern deconstructionism. The *Catechism of the Catholic Church* offers some statements about the natural moral law that I hold as classical Christian teaching, something that I wish Lutheran churches worldwide would have the wisdom to affirm. If that would have happened the ELCA would never have adopted its theologically heterodox "Social Statement on Human Sexuality" in 2009.

Here are some statements from the Catholic Catechism: "The natural law expresses the original sense which enables man to discern by reason the good and evil, the truth and the lie." Another: "The natural law states the first and essential precepts which govern moral life." Still another: "The natural law, present in the heart of each man and established by reason, is universal in its precepts and its authority extends to all men. It expresses the dignity of the person and determines the basis for his fundamental rights and duties."[101]

The Lutheran dogmatic tradition has taken the substance of the natural law into its doctrine of the orders of creation, thus linking it more to biblical than to philosophical conceptuality. This doctrine maintains that Christians along with all other human beings participate in universal structures that exist prior to and apart from the Bible and Christian teaching. God has placed all human beings in particular structures of existence, such as ethnicity, sexuality, family, work, and government. The law of God and his commandments are revealed through these common forms of human existence and function apart from the gospel and faith in Christ. God works through the law engraved in the nature of the things he creates. God is universally present as the pressure that drives people to do what they must do to sustain life, to administer justice, and to care for their families. The next time you hear the alarm clock, and your conscience tells you to get up, you lazy bum, that is the voice of the hidden God you are hearing.

Natural law is the enemy of cultural relativism, the notion that laws are mere moral conventions that vary among societies, with no basis in the way things are constituted. That would relegate the ideal of justice to the oscillating opinions of human beings. The law of justice must be the same for everyone, so that if murder and rape are morally wrong in America, they are equally so in Asia. Torture is wrong no matter who tries to excuse it. Humans have a God-given right to freedom and equality that should be universally respected and defended. Moral convictions such as these cannot be derived from the gospel. The gospel is not "written on human hearts," but comes from the outside, always by means of the external word (*verbum externum*). A high evaluation of the natural moral law does not detract from the integrity and uniqueness of the gospel. Law and gospel are both from the same God, but their purposes are utterly different. Natural law or the law of creation refers to the way God administers the world order "between the times," between the fall and the *parousia*. Its use is limited to the conditions of historical existence on the way to the final judgment and consummation. In the eschatological kingdom the earthly orders will be transfigured into a new creation. There will no longer be any need for the law.

The purpose of this chapter has been to present an interpretation of Christian ethics in light of the biblical concept of the kingdom of God. How to apply this approach to a plethora of moral problems would be important and interesting, but that would call for the writing of another book. Perhaps enough has been said to show that without the footing of natural law, Christian ethics would have to hobble along on one leg. It would have virtually nothing to say about such controversial issues as capital punishment, pacifism, just war theory, weapons of mass destruction, contraception, abortion, euthanasia, eugenics, cloning, stem cell research, universal health care, global warming, deviations of sexual behavior, and the like. Furthermore, only high level commissions would have the expertise to deal responsibly with all these moral issues, and that is most certainly beyond the competence of any single person.

Chapter Six
Eschatology

Some aspects of the eschatology to be found in Luther's writings or the Lutheran Confessions in the *Book of Concord* can no longer be maintained by Lutherans today. This is equally true of other traditions from the Reformation era, Reformed (John Calvin) and Anabaptist (Thomas Müntzer). For Luther was not unique in believing that his generation was living in apocalyptic times, expecting the end of the world to come at any time soon. Luther was a serious reader of the Bible, actually a learned professor of Holy Scripture. He translated the Bible from its original languages and wrote many exegetical commentaries. Luther thought he learned from the prophecies of Ezekiel that the world would end in his lifetime. He thought he learned from Paul's writings to the Thessalonians that the pope was the Anti-Christ, and he repeated it many times. Luther's study of the Bible convinced him that the invasion of the Turks was a sign that the day of judgment was imminent. Since history was soon coming to an end, there was no point to get involved to improve the social order. The whole society was disintegrating. The Turks were coming, the Peasants were rebelling, the Catholic Church was corrupt, and the Protestants were disunited. Luther's eschatology was the reason for his quietism in social and political thought. Only God holds in his hand the solution to all human problems. Ever since then the shadow of Luther's conservatism has cast itself upon all subsequent centuries of Lutheran history. Someone has joked that the Lutheran Church is the Republican Party at prayer. That is a characterization that no longer holds.

The Last Things in the Lutheran Tradition

The Lutheran *Book of Concord* passes along some of Luther's typical eschatological ideas, particularly his belief in the imminence of the Last Day. The world is growing old and we are living in its last days. The world is experiencing the throes of a violent rebellion against God, as evidenced by the kingdom of the Anti-Christ and the kingdom of Mohammed. The Confessions have a lot to say about the Anti-Christ, even identifying him as the pope.

There is only one article that deals explicitly with eschatology, Article 17 of the *Augsburg Confession*, entitled "Concerning the Return of Christ to Judgment." It is worth quoting in full:

> It is also taught that our Lord Jesus Christ will return on the Last Day to judge, to raise all the dead, to give eternal life and eternal joy to those who believe and are elect, but to condemn the ungodly and the devils to hell and eternal punishment. Rejected, therefore, are the Anabaptists who teach that the devils and condemned human beings will not suffer eternal torture and torment. Likewise rejected are some Jewish teachings, which have also appeared in the present, that before the resurrection of the dead saints and righteous people alone will possess a secular kingdom and will annihilate all the ungodly.

These statements commit Lutherans to the following beliefs: 1) the return of Christ, 2) the final judgment, 3) the universal resurrection, 4) eternal life for the elect, 5) and eternal damnation for the lost. This confession rejects the idea of universal salvation, that everyone will be saved in the end, apparently taught by some Anabaptists at the time. It also rejects the idea of a millennium, the belief in a thousand year kingdom on earth ruled by the saints.

In traditional dogmatics the final chapter covered eschatology, under the rubric of "The Last Things." The seventeenth century orthodox Lutheran theologians provided further development and refinement of the eschatological statements they received from Luther and the Lutheran confessional writings.[102] However, their ideas were remarkably consistent with the mainstream thinking of Roman Catholicism, except for their criticism of the medieval theory of the five places people are sent when they die: 1) hell, for the unbelieving and unrepentant wicked people; 2) purgatory, for Christians who have not been purged of venial sins and have not given full satisfaction for punishments due to sin; 3) limbo of infants, for children who die before they are baptized; 4) limbo of the fathers, for the patriarchs of the Old Testament who died before the descent of Christ to hell to deliver them into a state of heavenly bliss; 5) heaven, for all the saints purged of sin. The Lutherans were particularly adamant about rejecting the idea of purgatory because of its conflict with the doctrine of justification by faith alone. They also rejected the two limbos because of their lack of scriptural support. The Old and the New Testaments teach only two final terminals, heaven and hell.

The orthodox Lutheran theologians gave the traditional Christian answer to the question, "What happens when a person dies?" When death happens, the soul separates from the body and never dies. The body is interred and turned to dust. Lutherans taught the immortality of the soul, a doctrine more at home in Greek philosophy than in biblical theology. The pagan belief in the immortality of the soul was ingeniously amalgamated with the Christian belief in the resurrection of the body. The body that dies will be resurrected and reunited with the soul, but without sensing any need for food, sleep, or sex. They will be "spiritual bodies," as the apostle Paul says. The new bodies with the same old souls will be like the angels, shining with heavenly light and glory. The extreme pains and sufferings of the wicked in eternal hell are depicted in gruesome detail, in contrast to the ineffable joys and blessings of everlasting life with God in heaven.

The final judgment follows immediately after the resurrection of all the dead. Some will still be living at that time, so their souls will not be separated from their bodies. No one knows when the final judgment will take place. Lutherans are not among those who make predictions about the end of the world. Christ will sit on the throne of judgment deciding the eternal fate of the blessed and the damned, according to the revealed norms of God's law and gospel. Although no one knows the exact time, there are signs that precede the end of the world, but Lutherans are counseled not to indulge in futile speculations. In particular they reject the speculations of the Chiliasts or Millennialists who teach that Christ will return to earth and set up a thousand year kingdom in which the saints will be endowed with perfect knowledge of God, martyrs will rise from the dead, the Jews will be converted, and the anti-Christ will be overthrown. These ideas are based on arbitrary interpretation of prophecies in the *Book of Revelation*, the last book in the Bible and the least understood by its readers.

The Rediscovery of Eschatology

Since the Reformation eschatology has been the happy hunting ground of mystics, numerologists, and gnostics who search the Scriptures for esoteric meanings about future events and the last things. In contrast, Reformation Protestants and Roman Catholics have been content to warn against relying on the magic of numbers and instead teach the basics of their catechisms. For the most part orthodox theologians have avoided macrocosmic speculations about the end times, and focused their attention more on the microcosmic eschatology that pertains to each individual facing his or her own death. After all, most Christians are more concerned about preparing for their own personal demise than about the end of the world that seems extremely remote.

The problem with placing eschatology in the last chapter of dogmatics is that it assumed an increasingly stagnant life of its own, without any explicit connection to what went before. Eschatology was treated like an appendix of dogmatics, split off from the existential core of its soteriology, the person and work of Christ and the way of salvation (*ordo salutis*). There, in the last chapter, it languished in a moribund state, offering little guidance or relevance for pastors and priests who must preach and preside at the funerals of their parishioners. Then something dramatic happened in twentieth century theology. Eschatology made a comeback with passion and power to transform the method and content of Christian thought. This was brought about by the spin-off effects of two epoch-making books: *The Preaching of Jesus Concerning the Kingdom of God*, by Johannes Weiss,[103] and *The Quest of the Historical Jesus*, by Albert Schweitzer.[104] From their point of view they were merely engaged in a scholarly project of historical research. What did Jesus mean by the kingdom of God? They had no idea they were igniting dynamite sticks at the foundation of the regnant liberal Protestant theology of the nineteenth century. Post-Enlightenment Christianity had become a synthesis of religion and society, based on the idea of the Kingdom of God on earth being realized through moral and spiritual progress, chiefly through the actions of love and the pursuit of justice by people of good will. The books by Weiss and Schweitzer had a shattering effect on the pillar on which liberal Christianity was based. They demonstrated that the kingdom of God in Jesus' preaching did not refer to the construction of a new social order which humans can build in partnership with God. Rather, the kingdom is the power of God breaking in from above as a great crisis and act of renewal.

Immediately on the heels of this shift from an ethical to an eschatological concept of the kingdom of God, virtually every theologian thereafter had to put this new hypothesis into play. Karl Barth seized the moment with his assertion: "Christianity that is not entirely and altogether eschatology has entirely and altogether nothing to do with Christ."[105] Eschatology was no longer a topic reserved for the concluding chapter of dogmatics. Instead of being postponed to the "last things," eschatology deals with the "first things." Eschatology permeates the whole of the Christian faith and it lies at the beginning of Christian theology. Still, theologians could not reach any consensus on many questions. Indeed, we can discern at least five different schools of thought on how to interpret eschatology.

1) *Thoroughgoing eschatology.* This is the common label for the views of Schweitzer and Weiss. They were adopted by two liberal Protestant theologians in Switzerland, Martin Werner and Fritz Buri. They accepted the idea of Schweitzer and Weiss that Jesus held an apocalyptic eschatology, believing that the kingdom of God would be ushered in by a catastrophic judgment. The world was coming to a fiery end in the very near future. However, we know the end did not come as Jesus expected. They said that Jesus was proved wrong by history and that his eschatology was bound up with a primitive world view that is now outdated and irrelevant for people living today. Schubert Ogden, a leader of process thought, is the one American theologian who appropriated Fritz Buri's ideas at face value. The result was a theology that surrendered the uniqueness and universality of Jesus Christ.

2) *Realized eschatology.* This represents the position of C. H. Dodd and some Anglican theologians, most notably George Caird and N. T. Wright. In this view the kingdom of God is not eschatologically future but already fully present in the church and its sacraments. Their *locus classicus* is the passage in Luke's Gospel, "The kingdom of God is in the midst of you" (Lk. 17: 21). The problem with this idea is that the future is treated as a meaningless epilogue to the present. Dodd interprets the sayings which refer to the future as pointing symbolically to a transcendent spiritual world beyond time and space, shades of neo-Platonism.

3) *History-of-salvation eschatology. Heilsgeschichte* is the German term for the "history of salvation." This position was represented by Joachim Jeremias, George Kümmel, and Oscar Cullmann. Their intention was to take into account both the present and future aspects of the kingdom in the teaching of Jesus. Jeremias coined the phrase, "*sich realisierende Eschatologie* (eschatology in the process of being realized). The drama of salvation unfolds in a way that keeps the tension between the "already" and the "not yet." Salvation has *already* arrived in the person and ministry of Jesus but it has *not yet* reached its final fulfillment. The eschatological end of history

186

is still outstanding. The church lives and carries out the mission of Christ between the times, between the occurrence of salvation in history and the great transformation above and beyond history.

4) *Existentialist eschatology.* Rudolf Bultmann created a concept of eschatology sans *eschaton.* For him eschatology does not refer to an objective future end of history. Jesus' apocalyptic eschatology is demythologized so as to have reference to an ultimately significant moment in which a person experiences the crisis of God's judgment and has an opportunity to decide for authentic existence. The forgiveness of sins announced by the *kerygma* (the gospel) is an eschatological event. Existence in faith is eschatological existence here and now. The end-time is the *kairos* in which the decision for life or death hangs in the balance. To the eyes of faith any moment might be experienced as the fulness of time. Bultmann believed that his radical conversion of eschatology into each existential encounter in the present moment can be supported by the letters of Paul and the Gospel of John. All the passages that refer to the past or future are written off as remnants of apocalyptic Judaism or additions of the later church. Nothing remains but the existential category of the present moment in which the events of judgment and mercy, faith and love, occur through the kerygmatic proclamation.

5) *Dialectical eschatology.* The dominant motif of this type of eschatology is the dialectical relation between time and eternity. The writings of the early Barth (e.g., in his *Romans Commentary*), Paul Althaus' book on eschatology, *Die letzten Dinge* (1922), and the third volume of Paul Tillich's *Systematic Theology* are representative of this approach. Eschatology does not deal with the future ending of history. The last things are the ultimate things that concern human beings, matters of conscience rather than chronology. Each and every person is equidistant from eternity. Eschatology has to do with the transcendent meaning of each moment in a person's life. Eternity is above and beyond time and therefore always contemporary. With each passing year we are not getting closer to the end of

time and history. The end is the quality of eternity breaking in suddenly from above. The source of this way of thinking about the dialectic of eternity and time is German idealism. The present moment is the bearer of eternal meaning (the *nunc aeternum*). The category of the future never receives its due in the conceptuality of dialectical theology. The future tense, however, is essential in the biblical story of salvation, couched in the language of promise and fulfillment, the language of hope and expectation. Eschatology that does not focus on the future yet to happen cannot give expression to the hope of faith. Paul wrote that we "groan inwardly while we wait for adoption, the redemption of our bodies. For in hope we were saved. Now hope that is seen is not hope. For who hopes for what is seen? But if we hope for what we do not see, we wait for it with patience" (Rom. 8: 23b-25).

Eschatology: The Future of Hope

Protestant theology after World War II was dominated by the rivalry and competition between two theological camps, the Barthians and the Bultmannians. Heinrich Ott made an effort to combine the christological emphasis of Barth and the herme-neutical approach of Bultmann into one system of theology. It proved to be a mish-mash that lacked consistency and was soon dismissed by critics as a marriage of ideas not made to last. Then the new theology of hope came upon the scene and pro-vided a way forward beyond the stalemate between the Barthians and the Bultmannians. Wolfhart Pannenberg and Jürgen Moltmann, the two leaders of this movement, took the rediscovery of eschatology post-Schweitzer in a new direction. Two of their books set forth the principles of their eschatological theology of the hope and the future of human-ity and the world, Moltmann's *Theology of Hope*[106] and Pannenberg's *Revelation as History*.[107] I wrote my first contri-bution to further the development of this new program, en-titled *The Future of God*.[108] At the same time my friend and colleague, Robert W. Jenson, offered his rendition of theology in the key of eschatology, entitled *The Knowledge of Things Hoped For.*[109]

We have indicated that some theologians, notably Buri and Bultmann, accepted Schweitzer's verdict that Jesus' eschatological concept of the kingdom of God was trapped in the outdated categories of Jewish apocalypticism, and was therefore no longer relevant to modern people. Pannenberg and Moltmann disagreed. The alleged hermeneutical gap between Jesus' eschatology and modern culture can be bridged by taking up the category of hope and the future common to both. In this way the world view of the Bible can be brought into contact with the existential situation of modern people. The eschatological horizon of the Bible and the orientation of secular culture share a concern for the future of individual human beings in particular and of world historical trends in general. Theology does not need to go it alone to point out possible border crossings between a biblical eschatology of hope and a secular philosophy of hope.

Ernst Bloch[110] and Frederick Polak[111] are two secular authors who have written brilliantly on the categories of hope and the future that have proved to be of apologetic usefulness for the renewal of eschatological theology. Ernst Bloch made an ontological assertion that makes a lot of biblical sense: "The real genesis is not at the beginning, but at the end."[112] In the beginning when God created the world, he fore-knew how things would come to pass at the end. The half-blindfolded God of process philosophy does not resemble the God of the Bible. The Christian faith began with the in-breaking of the *eschaton*. The end of God's way with humanity became history in the incarnation of God and created a new beginning in the resurrection of Jesus. To do theology and ethics by beginning with eschatology is a proposal to take seriously our Lutheran emphasis on the *solus Christus*. Taking seriously the uniqueness of Jesus and his apocalyptic eschatology leads to an understanding of reality as history, of hope as essentially human, of revelation as promise, and of God as the power of the absolute future. Ernst Käsemann said it well: "Apoca-

189

lypticism was the mother of all Christian theology."[113] Theologians who try to forgive Jesus his eschatological trespasses lose his decisive meaning for a contemporary understanding of the Christian faith.

Early Christianity proclaimed Jesus' eschatological message of the kingdom of God as the goal of human hope. Believers continue to pray each day, "Thy kingdom come!" We look to the future for God to intervene in a powerful way to change things as they are. Jesus made the claim that a person's relation to the future coming of God's kingdom is determined by his or her relation to himself. The eschatological kingdom of God became a real presence in Jesus' personal life and ministry without ceasing to be future. Two thousand years later believers in Jesus are still living in a period of tension between the "already" and the "not yet." The kingdom-of-God tradition in Christianity has been preserved in early Christian chiliasm, Montanism, Joachimism, Anabaptism, millennialist Pietism, and Pentecostalism. From a Lutheran perspective the dialectic between the past-historical realization of the kingdom of God in the incarnation of Christ (the *ephapax*) and his sacramental presence in the church and the final advent of Christ ushering in the end of the world has been one-sidedly collapsed in favor of the apocalyptic future in these movements. When existence "between the times" is experienced as utterly miserable and unbearable, the apocalyptic imagination is revived to inspire radical Christian groups to long for the rapture and leave this messy world behind.

Immanuel Kant, the great philosopher of the Enlightenment, asserted that there are three questions of paramount rational significance: What can I know? What ought I to do? What may I hope? Science answers the first question, morality the second, and religion the third. Ernst Bloch, the philosopher of hope, wrote: "Where there is hope, there is religion."[114] Lutheranism has majored in the language of faith and love,[115] but has only minored in the language of hope. Lutheranism, a reforming movement, needs to recover the biblical story of a covenant people, who walk by hope toward a promised land.

190

Of course, Lutheran Orthodoxy did have a theology of hope and the future, but by placing it among the "last things" of eschatology in the last chapter of dogmatics, students went to sleep before they got to the end. It was a matter of too little too late. The phenomena of hope and the future belong at the beginning of the Christian faith because the gospel of the crucified and risen Lord Jesus is the final answer to the human quest for life and salvation.

The Bible is full of the promises of God, starting with Adam and Eve and continuing with Abraham and the patriarchs. The God of Israel revealed himself as a God of history and hope. The Old Testament records the history of God's struggle to keep his people from hankering to return to the flesh pots of the past or to stay in the present. The life of Abraham, as Paul told it, was an exercise of hope. Abraham, the father of many nations, kept on hoping "when hope seemed hopeless" (Rom. 4: 18). Abraham was promised a son, but Sarah's condition seemed hopeless. He left his country, kinfolk, and father's house and walked with unarmed obedience and trust in the word of promise. The story of hope and the future continued with Moses. His people were in slavery with no reasonable hope for liberation. But unexpectedly a leader arose to lead an exodus from slavery and oppression. The features of this story became landmarks on the way to the Jewish hope for a Messiah. The wayfaring people of the exodus who moved forward with a lively hope for a land flowing with milk and honey in the meantime were provided with enough manna for the day-to-day journey. Israel's sin was to despair of the promise of God and to settle for the immediate satisfaction a golden calf can give. "Despair" comes from the Latin "de-sperare," meaning "without hope."

The story of Israel continued with the prophets. Their message was of God's judgment but not without hope for deliverance. The prophetic message was that the God of Israel is the God of hope, but not only for Israel but ultimately for all the nations. The hope of Israel expanded even further in the encounter with death. The power of God was affirmed against all the boundaries of life, even the last, death itself. But the Old Testament does not provide a sure and certain hope in the face of death. It leaves a space open to be filled in by later history, not knowing that hope beyond death would be given a new foundation by God in raising Jesus from the grave.

The story of Jesus in the New Testament is told within the horizon of Israel's eschatological hope. After the crucifixion of Jesus one of the two disciples (possibly Cleopas) on the road to Emmaus said, "We had hoped that he was the one to redeem Israel" (Lk. 24: 21). On trial before King Agrippa, Paul testified, "I stand here on trial on account of my hope in the promise made by God to our ancestors, a promise that our twelve tribes hope to attain, as they earnestly worship day and night. It is for this hope, your Excellency, that I am accused by Jews. Why is it thought incredible by any of you that God raises the dead?" (Acts: 26: 6-8). For the apostle Paul the promise and the future of hope are solidly founded on the resurrection of Jesus.

The Resurrection of Jesus as an Eschatological Event

The resurrection of Jesus is the eschatological event of salvation history recorded in Holy Scripture. The resurrection of all the dead is what many Jews, particularly the Pharisees, expected would happen at the end of time, just before the final judgment when God will separate the sheep from the goats. The death of Jesus is the terminal point of his life; the resurrection is a new beginning, showing forth the power of God to put to death the last enemy of humankind. In Jesus' resurrection the eschatological future of life beyond death entered the realm of the dying and overcame the deadliness of death inside its stronghold.

If the life of Jesus had ended with his crucifixion, not to be followed by his resurrection, the hope of Israel for a Messiah would have been dashed. The testimony of the apostles and the early church would have made no sense if their claim that Jesus was the Messiah had not been vindicated by his resurrection from the dead. Jews would not have pinned their hopes on a dead Messiah. Apart from his resurrection Jesus' claim to speak with authority for God would have disqualified him as just another messianic pretender. Some act of legitimation was needed to counter the condemnation of Jesus for blasphemy by the Jewish authorities.

The resurrection of Jesus was the first fruits, a down payment, on what God has in store for the whole of humanity and the world when history comes to its final end. Many more things would need to happen before it could be said that the kingdom of God was fully realized. The salvation the Messiah promised is real but partial. Poor, sick, and hungry persons are still with us, and the reign of peace, joy, freedom, and righteousness is still a dream.

Of crucial importance is the Christian belief that the resurrection of Jesus really happened as a bodily event in history, in space and time. If it did not really happen, preachers would be fools to talk about it on Easter Sunday. But many do. Why? Because they have bought into the Gnostic idea that the body counts for nothing, only the spirit matters. New Testament scholar, Marcus Borg,[116] is the darling of such Gnostic preachers of which there happen to be legion. For them the resurrection is a spiritual event, something that happens within one's soul apart from the body. Orthodox Christians believe in the "resurrection of the body," because the body stands for the whole person (*pars pro toto*). Without a body a person would be no-body. Paul says, Jesus was raised a "spiritual body" (I Cor: 15: 44), different from the physical body we indwell, but surely in some way continuous with it. We possess no theory to explain the event of Jesus' resurrection from the grave. Just as God had the power to create the world out of nothing (*creatio ex nihilo*), so also he has the power to create new life out of death. The total personal being of Jesus of Nazareth was transformed to a new mode of reality into which by the grace of God we are initiated through faith and baptism.

What we do know is that the resurrection of Jesus was an eschatological event that occurred in history before the end of time. As such this event generates hope for life beyond death for all those who place their future in the hands of the living God who raised Jesus from the dead. Jesus is the pioneer of hope because he overcame the deadly power of death once for all, by being raised into union with God the Father who creates something from nothing and life from death. When the women and the disciples saw the crucified Jesus alive after his entombment, they had to make a decision. Either this was a miracle of revivification, in which case Jesus, like Lazarus, would have to face death again, or this was really the eschatological event of resurrection, something they were anticipating to occur beyond death, the language for which was ready made in late-Jewish apocalypticism. The resurrection of Jesus is not merely an answer to the question whether a person who dies can live again; it is also an affirmation that the crucified Jesus now lives in union with God, not only for himself, but as our representative who has gone ahead to prepare the way for us. This event is the reason we can look to Jesus as our Judge, Savior and Lord. If we took away this event from the structure of Christian faith, we would still be standing in the Old Testament situation, looking for the Messiah to come. We would have no Christ; the cause for which Jesus lived and gave his life as a sacrifice for others would have died with him; and there would be no Christianity as we know it. Without belief in the resurrection, faith and Jesus would fall apart because God and Jesus would fall apart. Then, keeping Jesus at the center of worship would be nothing but pious idolatry.

Because God has raised Jesus from the dead, we have sufficient reason to hope for eternal life. There can be no gospel without it. The resurrection of Jesus is the good news of "in spite of." In spite of the jaws of death that will swallow all of us in the end, in spite of the negative experiences of emptiness and failure that bring doubt and despair now, we are given reason to "hope against hope" because of Christ. We know we have to die, yet on account of Christ we hope and trust that the word of life is stronger than the fate of death. We hope for a lasting future of our personal identity, as well as life together with all those whom we have embraced in love. Occasionally pastors encounter people who say that death is no big deal. I do not believe them. They are lying — not unusual for people doing everything they can to cheat death. Modern people show signs of being just as scared of death as ancient and medieval people. Otherwise, why are morticians paid a lot of money to make a dead person look life-like? Why do they give a corpse an expensive ride to the cemetery in a big black limousine? Why do we use euphemisms to refer to dying like "passing on" and "going home"?

Resurrection hope concerns the individual person, but its scope is wider. There is a universalism of hope, embracing the future of society, the world, and all things (*ta panta*) (Col. 1: 20). At the end God will be "all in all," totally present in everyone and everything (I Cor. 15: 28). The apostle Paul's vision of hope is magnificent and mind-boggling. Communal and cosmic dimensions are included, far transcending hope for the salvation of individual souls. Christians imbued with the love of God hope not merely for themselves, their family and friends, but for all those for whom Christ died and was resurrected for the world's redemption. As Christians we live in solidarity with the whole family of humankind and the whole of creation. Eschatological fulfillment incorporates personal and social aspects. When one member suffers, the whole body of humanity is in pain. Nor can the natural world be excluded from the vision of eschatological hope. The history of nature is also heir to the promise of fulfillment. The gospel is not good news for people and bad news for the rest of creation. According to Paul's eschatological vision, the forward movement of the material world and of personal and social life converge on the same ultimate destiny, the reconciliation of all things to God (*apokatastasis tōn pantōn*).

Article 17 of the *Augsburg Confession* rejects the idea of universal salvation. Neither Luther nor the Confessions teach that the devil and his ilk will be saved in the end. Sinners are all headed for damnation, deserving of the wrath and judgment of God, unless and until they have been born again by faith in Christ. The Confessions are also clear in rejecting the Calvinist idea of double predestination, whether for eternal salvation or eternal damnation. There is a difference between teaching that all *will* be saved in the end (universal salvation), and *praying* that God in his mercy will save all those who in the end come to trust in Christ for their salvation. Many persons have lived and died without ever coming within earshot of any voice of the gospel. We do not know what God will do about that. Some theologians have found meaning in the passage in I Peter 3: 18-20a: "For Christ also suffered for sins once for all, the righteous for the unrighteous, in order to bring you to God. He was put to death in the flesh, but made alive in the spirit, in which also he went and made a proclamation to the spirits in prison, who in former times did not obey." This proclamation was made to people who lived in the days of Noah; who else was there to hear we do not know. But it may be, as some have speculated, that God was giving people a *post-mortem* second chance. It is wonderful that we do not need to decide such matters. We can afford to remain gloriously agnostic about things we have no way of knowing. The point is this — whatever our speculations, we are bound to observe our three-dimensional confessional canon that teaches salvation *sola gratia, per fidem, propter Christum.*

Endnotes

Chapter One

1. Jn. 15: 16.
2. Rom. 8: 30.
3. I Tim. 2: 4.
4. See *Union with Christ, The New Finnish Interpretation of Luther*, eds., Carl E. Braaten and Robert W. Jenson (Grand Rapids, MI: Wm. B. Eerdmans Publishing Co., 1998).
5. The three Synods that merged in 1917 to form the Norwegian Lutheran Church in America were: The Hauge Synod, reflecting pietistic low church concerns and lay leadership, the Norwegian Synod, with leanings toward the Missouri Synod, was strong on church order and confessional Lutheran doctrine, and the United Church, which was a mediating group that pushed hard for Lutheran unity, maintaining that the two rival interpretations of the doctrine of election could both be accepted as orthodox.
6. See, *Lehrverurteilungen-kirchentrennend? Rechtfertigung, Sakramente und Amt im Zeitalter der Reformation und heute*, ed. by Karl Lehmann and Wolfhart Pannenberg (Göttingen: Vandenhoek & Ruprecht, 1986).
7. *The Book of Concord, The Confessions of the Evangelical Lutheran Church*, edited by Robert Kolb and Timothy J. Wengert (Minneapolis: Fortress Press, 2000).
8. Heinrich Schmid, *The Doctrinal Theology of the Evangelical Lutheran Church*, trans. by Henry E. Jacobs and Charles E. Hay (Philadelphia: United Lutheran Publication House, 1875).
9. The contrast between two Evangelicals, Timothy George and Brian D. McLaren, illustrates the growing split in contemporary Evangelicalism.
10. Kent S. Knutson, former president of the American Lutheran Church, wrote his doctoral dissertation for Union Theological Seminary on the variety of ecclesiologies held by contemporary Lutheran theologians. See, Kent S. Knutson, *The Community of Faith and the Word: An Inquiry into the Concept of the Church in Contemporary Lutheranism* (New York: Union Theological Seminary, 1961).
11. See, Carl E. Braaten, *Because of Christ — Memoirs of a Lutheran Theologian* (Grand Rapids, MI: Wm. B. Eerdmans Publishing Co., 2010).
12. Lk. 10: 41-42.
13. Wolfhart Pannenberg, ed., *Offenbarung als Geschichte* (Göttingen, Germany: Vandenhoek & Ruprecht, 1961).
14. Rom. 3: 22b-23.
15. See the blog written by Dan Skogen, "Exposing the ELCA."

Chapter Two

16. II Cor. 11: 13.

17. II Cor. 12: 11.

18. Phil. 3: 2.

19. Gal. 3: 28.

20. James 2: 18 & 24.

21. Rom. 11: 17.

22. Quoted from Hans Joachim Kraus, *Geschichte des historisch-kritischen Erforschung des Alten Testaments von der Reformation bis zur Gegenwart* (Neukirchen: Verlag der Buchhandlung des Erziehungsvereins, 1956), p. 351.

23. Jn. 1: 1 & 14.

24. Philadelphia: Westminster Press, 1960.

25. Alfred Loisy, *The Gospel and the Church*, trans. Christopher Home (Philadelphia: Fortress Press, 1976), p. 166.

26. Lk. 24: 21.

27. I Cor. 15: 20.

28. Adolf von Harnack, *What Is Christianity?* trans. Thomas Bailey Saunders (New York: Harper & Brothers Publishers, 1957), p. 63.

29. Robert W. Funk, *Honest to Jesus* (San Francisco: Harper & Collins, 1996). John Dominic Crossan, *Jesus: A Revolutionary Biography* (San Francisco: Harper & Collins, 1994).

30. Robert W. Funk, *Honest to Jesus*, p. 301.

31. Mk. 16: 16.

32. Exod. 6: 6.

33. Rom. 11: 16.

34. I Cor. 3: 16.

35. I Cor. 14: 18-19.

36. I Cor. 12: 10.

37. Jürgen Moltmann, *The Trinity and the Kingdom*, trans. Margaret Kohl (San Francisco: Harper & Row, Publishers, 1981).

38. Jn. 14: 26.

39. Jn. 16: 13.

40. Jn. 16: 14.

41. Jn. 16: 15.

42. See Philip Jenkins, *The Next Christendom. The Coming of Global Christianity* (Oxford University Press, 2002).

43. In Latin, "*Sacramenta efficiunt quod significant et significant quod efficiunt.*"

44. Jn. 17: 21.

45. Matt. 16: 18.

46. Rom. 8: 39.

47. Rom. 12: 2.

48. Matt. 28: 20.

49. *Lumen Gentium*, no. 8.

50. St. Vincent was a fifth century monk in the monastery of Lérins. He coined the phrase, "*quod ubique, quod semper, quod ab omnibus.*"

51. St. Cyprian's assertion, "Outside the church there is no salvation," may be understood as a christological statement that salvation is exclusively the work of Christ mediated through the church. But to claim that salvation is the prerogative of one particular denomination is a case of sinful boasting.

52. Confessional Lutherans do not claim that their church is "*die allein selig machende Kirche,*" as some Catholic theologians have claimed for their church.

53. Dietrich Bonhoeffer, *Gesammelte Schriften*, Vol. 3 (Munich: Kaiser Verlag, 1966), p. 206.

54. Martin Luther, "On the Councils and the Church," *Luther's Works* (Concordia & Fortress, 1955), vol. 41, pp. 148-168.

55. Edmund Schlink, "Lord's Supper or Church's Supper," *Intercommunion.* Donald Baillie & John Marsh, eds. (London: SCM, 1952).

56. Matt. 16: 19.

57. Martin Luther, "On the Councils and the Church," *Luther's Works*, Vol. 41, p. 154.

58. I Cor. 12: 28.

59. Matt. 5: 11.

60. Rom. 10: 15.

61. Jaroslav Pelikan, *The Vindication of Tradition* (New Haven: Yale University Press, 1984), p. 65.

Chapter Three

62. John 17: 21.

63. "Apology of the Augsburg Confession," Article XXIV, *The Book of Concord*, eds. Robert Kolb & Timothy J. Wengert (Fortress Press, 2000), p. 261.

64. *Eucharist and Ministry*, p. 22.

65. *Eucharist and Ministry*, p. 32.

66. *Papal Primacy and the Universal Church*, p. 10.

67. *Teaching Authority and Infallibility in the Church*, p. 23.

68. Ibid., p. 25.

69. *Teaching Authority and Infallibility in the Church*, p. 58.

70. *Justification by Faith*, p. 74.

71. *Justification by Faith*, p. 16.

72. "Solid Declaration, Rule and Norm," Formula of Concord, *The Book of Concord*, Theodore Tappert, ed. (Fortress Press, 1959), p. 504.

73. John D. Zizioulas, *Being as Communion. Studies in Personhood and the Church* (Crestwood, NY: Vladimir Seminary Press, 1985).

74. J.-M. R. Tillard, *Church of Churches. The Ecclesiology of Communion* (Collegeville, MN: Liturgical Press, 1992).

75. Avery Dulles, *The Survival of Dogma* (New York: Doubleday & Company, 1971), p. 171.

76. Walter Kasper, "Present Day Problems in Ecumenical Theology," *Reflections*, Center of Theological Inquiry, Spring 2003, Vol. 6, 80-81.

Chapter Four

77. Martin Kähler, "*Die Mission — ist sie ein unentbehrlicher Zug am Christentum,*" *Schriften zu Christologie und Mission* (Munich: Chr. Kaiser, 1971), p. 190.

78. Quoted by Gustav Warneck, *Outline of a History of Protestant Missions* (New York: Fleming H. Revell, 1906), pp. 14-15.

79. Quoted by Ludwig Wiedemann, *Mission und Eschatologie* (Paderborn: Bonifacius, 1965), p. 11.

80. John Hick, *God Has Many Names* (Philadelphia: The Westminister Press, 1980).

81. Paul F. Knitter, *No Other Name?* (Maryknoll, NY: Orbis Books, 1985).

82. Vinoth Ramachandra, "A Brief Reflection on Edinburgh 2010," taken from the internet: www.edinburgh2010.org.

Chapter Five

83. Helmut Thielicke, *Theological Ethics*, Vol. I (Philadelphia: Fortress Press, 1966), p. 47.

84. Paul Ramsey, *Basic Christian Ethics* (New York: Charles Scribner's Sons, 1951), p. 41.

85. T. W. Manson, *Ethics and the Gospel* (New York: Charles Scribner's Sons, 1960), p. 65.

86. Amos Wilder, *Eschatology and Ethics in the Teaching of Jesus* (New York: Harper & Brothers, 1939).

87. Wolfhart Pannenberg, *Theology and the Kingdom of God* (Philadelphia: The Westminster Press, 1969).

88. Reported by Richard J. Neuhaus in his Introduction to Pannenberg's book, *Theology and the Kingdom of God*.

89. Joseph Fletcher, *Situation Ethics* (Philadelphia: Westminster Press, 1966).

90. "Letter to Diognetus," *The Apostolic Fathers*, 2nd ed., trans. J. B. Lightfoot and J. R. Hammer (Grand Rapids: Baker, 1989), 5, 1-10.

91. H. Richard Niebuhr, *Christ and Culture* (New York: Harper & Brothers, 1956).

92. Ernst Troeltsch, *The Social Teaching of the Christian Churches*, trans. Olive Wyon (New York: Macmillan Co., 1931), Vol. I, chap. 3, sec. 2.

93. Karl Barth, *This Christian Cause: A Letter to Great Britain from Switzerland*, trans. E. L. H. Gordon and George Hill (New York: Macmillan Co., 1941).

94. Anders Nygren, "Luther's Doctrine of the Two Kingdoms," *The Ecumenical Review*, I, No. 3 (Spring, 1949), 301-10.

95. Dietrich Bonhoeffer, *Ethics*, ed. by Eberhard Bethge, trans. Neville Horton Smith (New York: Macmillan Co., 1955).

96. Gerhard Ebeling, "The Necessity of the Doctrine of the Two Kingdoms," *Word and Faith*, trans. James W. Leitch (Philadelphia: Fortress Press, 1963).

97. Heinrich Bornkamm, *Luther's Doctrine of the Two Kingdoms in the Context of His Theology*, trans. Karl H. Hertz (Philadelphia: Fortress Press, 1966).

98. Karl Hertz, ed., *Two Kingdoms and One World* (Minneapolis: Augsburg Publishing House, 1976), pp. 83-84.

99. Quoted in Hertz, *Two Kingdoms and One World*, p. 184.

100. Hertz, *Two Kingdoms and One World*, p. 87.

101. *Catechism of the Catholic Church* (Liguori Publications, 1994), pp. 474-75.

Chapter Six

102. The more important dogmaticians in the period of Lutheran orthodoxy are: Johann Gerhard (1582-1637); Mathias Hafenreffer (1561-1617);

Johannes Andreas Quenstedt (1617-1688); Johann Wilhelm Baier (1647-1695); David Hollaz (1648-1713).

103. Johannes Weiss, *Jesus' Proclamation of the Kingdom of God* (London, SCM Press, 1971). German title: *Die Predigt Jesu vom Reiche Gottes* (Göttingen: 1892).

104. Albert Schweitzer, *The Quest of the Historical Jesus* (London: Adam & Charles Black, 1954). German original: 1906).

105. Karl Barth, *The Epistle to the Romans*, tr. by Edwyn C. Hoskyns (London: Oxford University Press, 1933), p. 314.

106. Jürgen Moltmann, *Theology of Hope, On the Ground and the Implications of a Christian Eschatology*, tr. James W. Leitch (London: SCM Press, 1967).

107. Wolfhart Pannenberg, *Revelation as History*, tr. David Granskiou (New York: The Macmillan Co., 1968).

108. Carl E. Braaten, *The Future of God: The Revolutionary Dynamics of Hope* (New York: Harper & Row, 1969).

109. Robert W. Jenson, *The Knowledge of Things Hoped For: The Sense of Theological Discourse* (New York: Oxford University Press, 1969).

110. Ernst Bloch, *Das Prinzip Hoffnung* (Frankfurt: Suhrkamp Verlag, 1959), Vol. III.

111. Fred L. Polak, *The Image of the Future*, tr. Elise Boulding (New York: Oceana Publications, 1961), Vols. I & II.

112. Ernst Bloch, *Das Prinzip Hoffnung*, Vol. III, p. 1628.

113. Ernst Käsemann, "Die Anfänge christlicher Theologie," *Exegetische Versuche und Besinnungen*, Vol. 2 (Göttingen: Vandenhoek und Ruprecht, 1964), p. 100.

114. Ernst Bloch, *Das Prinzip Hoffnung*, Vol. III, p. 1404.

115. Here are some examples: George W. Forell, *Faith Active in Love* (Minneapolis: Augsburg Publishing House, 1954); Anders Nygren, *Agape and Eros*, tr. Philip S. Watson (Philadelphia: The Westminster Press, 1953); Lennart Pinomaa, *Faith Victorious, An Introduction to Luther's Theology*, tr. Walter J. Kukkonen (Philadelphia: Fortress Press, 1963.

116. See, Marcus J. Borg, *Jesus: A New Vision* (San Francisco: Harper & Row, Publishers, 1988); and *Meeting Jesus Again for the First Time* (HarperSanFrancisco, 1994).

Index

Ramsey, Paul, 151
Rauschenbusch, Walter, 139, 152
Reeb, James, 164
Ritschl, Albrecht, 37, 98, 139
Rosenberg, Alfred, 170
Rosenius, Carl Olaf, 8
Ruotsalainen, Paavo, 8

Sabellius, 59
Sanders, E. P., 54
Schelderup, Kristian, 9
Schleiermacher, Friedrich, 34, 37, 98
Schlink, Edmund, 36, 38, 40, 89
Schmid, Heinrich, 32
Skydsgaard, K. E., 36
Smith, Joseph, 129
Söderblom, Nathan, 35, 85
Sohm, Rudolf, 164
Spener, Philip Jacob, 8, 32, 135
Staupitz, Johann von, 21

Tatian, 132
Tertullian, 34, 58, 129
Theophilus, 132
Thielicke, Helmut, 151
Thurneysen, Eduard, 38
Tillard, J-M. R., 112
Tillich, Paul, 14, 39, 107, 187
Torrance, Thomas, 38, 42
Troeltsch, Ernst, 137

Valentinus, 52
Vincent of Lerins, St., 199

Warfield, Benjamin, 129
Weiss, Johannes, 185-186

Werner, Martin, 186
Whitehead, Alfred North, 34
Wilder, Amos, 152
Wittgenstein, Ludwig, 34
Wright, N. T., 54, 186

Zinzendorf, Count Ludwig von, 8, 137
Zizioulas, John, 42, 112
Zwingli, Huldreich, 18-19, 38

15376774R00110

Made in the USA
Charleston, SC
31 October 2012